MUSIC OF THE UNITED STATES OF AMERICA

Richard Crawford, Editor-in-Chief

James Wierzbicki, Executive Editor

FLORENCE PRICE

SYMPHONIES NOS. 1 AND 3

Edited by Rae Linda Brown and Wayne Shirley

Recent Researches in American Music • Volume 66

Music of the United States of America • Volume 19

Published for the
American Musicological Society
by

A-R Editions, Inc.
Middleton, Wisconsin

Published by A-R Editions, Inc.
8551 Research Way, Suite 180
Middleton, Wisconsin 53562

Printed in the United States of America

ISBN-13 978-0-89579-638-7
ISBN-10 0-89579-638-4
ISSN 0147-0078

Frontispiece: Florence Price, c. 1940 (Photographer unknown; Florence Price Collection,
David W. Mullins Library, University of Arkansas, Fayetteville, Arkansas; used by
permission.)

Publication of this edition has been supported by a grant from the National Endowment for
the Humanities, an independent federal agency.

♾ The paper in this publication meets the minimum requirements of American National
Standard for Information Sciences—Permanence of Paper for Printed Library Materials,
ANSI Z39-48-1992.

To Florence Beatrice Smith Price who, through her perserverance
and commitment to musical excellence, continues to inspire us all.
To my son, William, who is a continued source of inspiration and joy.
To my sisters, Helaine and Carlene, and to my mother, who are my best friends.

—Rae Linda Brown

CONTENTS

FOREWORD

Music of the United States of America (MUSA), a national series of scholarly editions, was established by the American Musicological Society (AMS) in 1988. In a world where many nations have gathered their proudest musical achievements in published scholarly form, the United States has been conspicuous by its lack of a national series. Now, with the help of collaborators, the AMS presents a series that seeks to reflect the character and shape of American music making.

MUSA, planned to encompass forty volumes, is designed and overseen by the AMS Committee on the Publication of American Music (COPAM), an arm of the society's Publications Committee. The criteria foremost in determining its contents have been: (1) that the series as a whole reflect breadth and balance among eras, genres, composers, and performance media; (2) that it avoid music already available through other channels, duplicating only where new editions of available music seem essential; and (3) that works in the series be representative, chosen to reflect particular excellence or to represent notable achievements in this country's highly varied music history.

The American Musicological Society's collaborators in the national effort that has brought MUSA to fruition include the National Endowment for the Humanities in Washington, D.C., which has funded MUSA from its inception; Brown University's Music Department in Providence, Rhode Island, which provided the project's original headquarters; the University of Michigan School of Music, where, since 1993, MUSA has made its home; A-R Editions, Inc., the publisher on behalf of AMS, of the MUSA series; and the Society for American Music, which, through its representative to COPAM, has provided advice on the contents of MUSA.

Richard Crawford, Editor-in-Chief

ACKNOWLEDGMENTS

My interest in Florence Price began while completing my master's degree at Yale University. In 1979–80 I catalogued the music in the James Weldon Johnson Collection of Negro Arts and Letters in the Beinecke Rare Book Library.[1] It was there that I found some of Price's music, including the unpublished manuscript of the Symphony No. 3 in C Minor (1940). During my many trips to the Music Division of the Library of Congress, I met and talked with Wayne Shirley, whose passion for and knowledge of American and African-American music, were a decisive influence in my research.

Many years later, while considering dissertation topics, I talked with the late Professor Eileen Southern who encouraged me to consider a topic in African-American music. That conversation, at the annual AMS meeting in Boston in 1981, was the first of many we had over the years. How glad I am that I took her advice. Equally supportive in my investigation of Florence Price's music was Claude Palisca, my dissertation advisor at Yale University. At a time when American music dissertations were still a novelty at some universities, Professor Palisca enthusiastically championed my topic. To the late Professor Eileen Southern and late Professor Claude Palisca I owe my heartfelt gratitude. Their passion for research and the high standards that they set for our field has served as inspiration for me all of these years. They taught me to "keep digging" until I found what I was looking for and to never accept "it can't be found" as an excuse to give up on an important lead. Mostly, they taught me how important it is to love what you do.

There were numerous librarians, musicologists, and historians who helped me to gather information on Florence Price's life.[2] These include Deborra Richardson (Moorland-Spingarn Research Center, Howard University), Sharon Scott, Dorothy Lyles, and Edward Manney (Vivian Harsh Research Collection of Afro-American History and Literature, Carter G. Woodson Regional Library of the Chicago Public Library), Tom Dillard (Director of Special Collections, University of Arkansas, Fayetteville), Jeanne Morrow (New England Conservatory of Music Library), Marguerite L. Daly (New England Conservatory of Music), Jeanne Salathiel (Detroit Public Library), Willard B. Gatewood (University of Arkansas), Chester W. Williams

---

1. M.A. thesis, African American Studies, Yale University, 1980. Published as *Music, Printed and Manuscript, in the James Weldon Johnson Collection of Negro Arts and Letters*. New York: Garland Press, 1982.

2. The titles and positions are given as they were at that time.

(former dean, New England Conservatory of Music), and Robert Brubaker (Chicago Historical Society).

I also wish to thank the reference librarians and staffs of the Detroit Public Library (which conserves the papers of the Michigan WPA Symphony Orchestra), the E. Azalia Hackley Memorial Collection of Negro Music, Drama, and Dance (Detroit Public Library), the Chicago Public Library Music Division, the Beinecke Rare Book and Manuscript Library of Yale University, the Mullins Library Special Collections at the University of Arkansas, and the Music Division of the Library of Congress. Wayne Shirley was tireless in his help and I am grateful for his support and friendship. He found "missing" Price scores at the Library. He helped to decipher shorthand on some of the Library's notecards with regard to copyright information, and he read numerous versions of my various manuscripts. I also want to thank Suzanne Flandreau of the Center for Black Music Research, who found material even when I was not looking for it.

I am especially appreciative of the many colleagues, friends, and students of Florence Price and their sons and daughters who shared with me her musical scores, photographs, letters, scrapbooks, and memorabilia. It is her friends who have given life to this work by sharing their memories and mementos of her with me. These include Eleanor Price (no relation), Vera Flandorf, Orrin Clayton Suthern, II, Dr. Ruth Fouché, Verna Arvey (wife of William Grant Still), Mildred Hall (wife of Dr. Frederick Hall), Bernice Hall (daughter-in-law of Dr. Frederick Hall), Dr. Florence Stith, Eugenia Anderson, Bernice Skooglund, William Duncan Allen, and Valter Poole (conductor of the Michigan WPA Orchestra).[3] I am especially grateful to Judith Anne Still (daughter of William Grant Still), Josephine Harreld Love, Helen White, and Marion Ross, all of whom spent days and days with me helping to establish a framework for Florence Price's life and career. I thank them for their time and hospitality (in Flagstaff, Los Angeles, Detroit, Chicago, and Little Rock). From them, I learned about Florence Price, the mother, wife, and friend.

Thanks also go to Theodore Chadwick (great grandson of George Whitefield Chadwick, director of the New England Conservatory of Music, 1897–1930), who gave me permission to use materials from Chadwick's memoirs. Special appreciation goes to Lawrence Robinson, Florence Price's grandson, who shared with me wonderful stories of his grandmother. I also wish to thank Vicki J. Taylor Hammond and Timothy J. Taylor (Florence Price's grandchildren) for their permission to publish the musical scores, letters, and other materials.

Over these many years there have been numerous friends and colleagues who have helped me along the way—with suggested leads on information, with thoughts about how to organize material, and general words of wisdom. Thanks go to Mildred Denby Green, Calvert Johnson, Steven Ledbetter, Doris McGinty, Josephine Wright, Maurice Wheeler, Judith Tick, Adrienne Fried Block, Marsha Heizer, Carol Oja, Guy Ramsey, Samuel A. Floyd, Jr., Olly Wilson, Bill Brown, Vivian Perlis, Catherine Parsons Smith, James Wierzbicki, and, especially my friend Rich Crawford, who helped to shape this volume. A special thank you to Barbara Garvey Jackson, who shared with me her initial work on Florence B. Price and was a gracious host during my visit to Arkansas.

My work on Florence Price was supported by several fellowships and grants including the Dorothy Danforth Fellowship (Yale University), a Rackham Faculty Research Grant (University of Michigan), a Ford Foundation Postdoctoral Fellowship,

---

3. The transcription of my interview with Valter Poole (28 May 1983) is housed in the Archive of the Oral History Program of the Institute on the Federal Theater Project and New Deal Culture. Fairfax, Va.: George Mason University, 1–33.

Rae Linda Brown

an Institute of American Cultures Research Grant (University of California, Los Angeles), a University of California President's Fellowship, and a University of California, Irvine, Research Grant. Thank you to Jim Simmons, who transcribed all of the musical examples.

The MUSA editions of Price's Symphony no. 1 and Symphony no. 3 were inspired by the burgeoning interest in and performances of her music. As the small-scale compositions became more available (piano music, art songs, arrangements of spirituals, and chamber music), the number of performances across the nation, by students, amateur, and professional musicians, exploded. From those performances came recordings, further disseminating her music.[4]

Curiosity in the large-scale works increased and the demand for the orchestra music was insistent. While the need to create performing scores—conductor's scores and a full set of parts—for these symphonies was apparent, the challenge was daunting given the relative illegibility of the Symphony no. 1, in particular, which existed only in a manuscript copy. Working with graduate students at the University of California, Irvine, I was able to make a computer-generated conductor's (full) score and set of parts. Performances commenced immediately.

Subsequently I began working on a computer-generated conductor's score and a set of parts for the Symphony no. 3. About the same time, Wayne Shirley generated a set of orchestra parts which were used at the William Grant Still Festival in Flagstaff, where the Symphony no. 3 was heard for the first time in its entirely in more than forty years.

With each of the early orchestra performances, the conductor's score and orchestra parts were appropriately revised. It should be noted that these conductor's scores and orchestra parts for both the Symphony no. 1 and the Symphony no. 3 remain independent of the scholarly volume presented here. Nevertheless, at the outset of work on the MUSA edition, the full scores of the performing editions (not published) were consulted, and they offer a frame of reference and context for this volume. Wayne Shirley, who has provided the meticulous Apparatus, has more fully explained the exegesis of these editions in his Critical Commentary.

Florence Price's Symphony no. 1 and Symphony no. 3 have been performed throughout the United States and her music is increasingly gaining the recognition it richly deserves. Recent performances include those by the Savannah Symphony, the Albany (Georgia) Symphony, the Springfield (Missouri) Symphony, the Orchestra of the Plymouth Music Series (Minneapolis), the Camellia Symphony Orchestra (Sacramento), the Bay Area Women's Philharmonic Orchestra (San Francisco), the American Symphony Orchestra, the Lansing (Michigan) Symphony, and the Kalamazoo (Michigan) Symphony Orchestra, among others. Perhaps the most significant performances of the Symphony no. 1 were the January 1998 concerts of the Atlanta Symphony Orchestra's annual Martin Luther King Jr. birthday commemoration. Held in the historic Martin Luther King Chapel over two evenings for a combined audience of 5,000 people, the concerts were later broadcast over National Public Radio.

Further recognition of and appreciation for Price's orchestra music was achieved when the Women's Philharmonic recorded the Symphony no. 3 (after live concert performances of the work) with Apu Hsu, conductor, on Koch International in 2001. This recording also includes the orchestral works *The Oak* (1934) and the *Mississippi River Suite*.

Price's orchestral music has been well received. To date, there have been more than twenty recent performances, and these have often included pre-concert lectures on her

---

4. As of this writing, there are no fewer than twenty recordings of Price's music available, not including the recording of the Symphony no. 3 in C Minor.

life and music. Now, for the first time, with this scholarly publication of her orchestral scores, Price's large-scale compositions are available for all to study. It is our hope that Florence Price's name will be forever synonymous with American orchestral music and that she will be included among those pioneering voices, among African Americans and women musicians, who forged a unique and important path in our great history.

Rae Linda Brown
Loyola Marymount University
Los Angeles, California

LIFTING THE VEIL: THE SYMPHONIES OF FLORENCE B. PRICE

Rae Linda Brown

Florence B. Price was the most widely known African-American woman composer from the 1930s to the early 1950s. She achieved national recognition when her Symphony in E Minor was premiered in 1933 by the Chicago Symphony under the direction of Frederick Stock. That concert marked the first performance of a large-scale work by an African-American woman composer by a major American orchestra. By 1935 Price's accomplishments as concert pianist, organist, teacher, and composer were such that her activities were duly noted in the *Chicago Defender*, arguably the most widely read black newspaper in the United States.

Almost all of Florence's Price's nearly three hundred compositions were performed during her lifetime, though little of her music was published. She composed more than seventy teaching pieces for the piano (some published by McKinley Music, Theodore Presser, Carl Fisher, and Clayton F. Summy, among others) and more than twenty large-scale piano works (only one of them published during her lifetime), as well as music for piano, four hands and two pianos, four hands. There are more than twenty works for organ (including teaching pieces, music for service, and concert pieces) and a small number of chamber works, almost all of them concert works for professional players. Her nineteen works for orchestra include concert overtures, three concertos (two for violin and one for piano), four symphonies, and several suites and programmatic compositions. An accomplished pianist and organist, Price premiered many of her own works. Major ensembles of the Midwest, including the Chicago Symphony, the Michigan WPA Symphony Orchestra, and the Woman's Symphony Orchestra of Chicago, performed her orchestra scores.

Making up the largest portion of her oeuvre are the more than one hundred vocal compositions that include art songs, arrangements of spirituals, and examples of popular vocal music. Price's songs were regularly performed by a professional coterie of friends and colleagues in Chicago as well as by such leading concert singers of the day as Marian Anderson, Blanche Thebom, Roland Hayes, Abbie Mitchell, and Harry Burleigh.

Florence Price grew up in Little Rock during the institutionalized racism of the post-Reconstruction period, was educated in New England, returned to the South to teach in Atlanta and Little Rock, and—like tens of thousands of other African Americans—ultimately moved to Chicago. There she established her career, and there she died in 1953. Price's exploration of self came about over a long period of time and was ultimately realized through her music: as a teacher, performer, and composer. Marginalized in her occupation by gender and race, Price persevered, and her story is not one of defeat but one of triumph specific to African-American women.

FLORENCE BEATRICE PRICE (1887–1953)

Florence Beatrice Smith Price was born in Little Rock, Arkansas, in 1887, during the post-Reconstruction years. Dr. James H. Smith, Florence Beatrice's father, was one of the most respected black men in Little Rock. He was a published author, teacher, inventor, and dentist. Born in Delaware in 1843 to free parents of mixed racial blood, Smith received his professional training in Philadelphia by working as an apprentice to white dentists. He was truly a pioneer in the field. Before 1880 there were fewer than one dozen legal black dentists in the United States. Like Smith, most blacks were denied entrance to colleges, so they entered the profession through white offices, where they served as laboratory technicians and apprentices to white doctors and attended their black patients. At the close of the Civil War Dr. Smith set up practice in Pittsburgh and after one year moved to Chicago, setting up his office in the heart of the city in the area known as The Loop. Dr. Smith's practice was a lucrative one, but he lost everything in the Great Fire of 1871. Rather than starting again from scratch, he headed south to Arkansas with a group of other black Chicagoans.

Teaching provided Dr. Smith with the income needed to purchase new instruments. He founded several schools for black children in rural Arkansas and for seven years he taught at night in two country schoolhouses. Building schools and educating blacks during Reconstruction, in the backwoods of Arkansas, was no easy task. In Smith's first novel, *Maudelle*, he described the rural teaching situation this way:

> The scenes presented in these night schools were such as to fill the human heart with sympathy too deep for expression in anything but tears. The school building was nothing more than an old log hut, twenty feet square, with no windows and only one door not high enough to admit a common-sized person without his stooping. The seats were simply logs, hewn on two sides; one of which furnished the seat, and the other, turned to the floor, kept the log in place. Into this primitive school-room sixty or seventy people crowded every night. . . . Many of the pupils had already grown gray in age, and misshapen in form, in the service of the white race. Night after night these old people wrestled with their letters, cheered on by the hope that they might learn to read God's word before death overtook them; and they were rewarded with that much learning and more, although many of them were between the ages of fifty and eighty years.[1]

In 1878, now married and starting a family, Dr. Smith resumed his dental practice. For over twenty years he was Little Rock's leading dentist for black and white patients (until the "Jim Crow" laws established legal segregation in the 1890s), and his patients included one of the state's governors. Of the eleven dentists listed in the Little Rock city directory at the turn of the twentieth century, Dr. Smith was the only black. [2]

---

1. Dr. James H. Smith, *Maudelle: A Novel Founded on Facts Gathered from Living Witnesses* (Boston: Mayhew Publishing, Co., 1906), 6. *Maudelle* is a fact-based work, though not an autobiography, written as a powerful attack on the system of slavery. Maudelle is a mulatto, who, after being held in bondage, is released and works during her lifetime for the rights of the disenfranchised. The tragic mulatto story or moralist drama has a long tradition in African-American literature. One of the earliest novels on this subject was William Wells Brown's *Clotel: or the President's Daughter*, published in 1853. Moral uplift of the race through education continued to be a common theme for black writers through the turn of the century. This subject found its way into musical sources as well. The best-known example is Scott Joplin's opera *Treemonisha*.

2. Information on Dr. Smith may be found in several sources. Among them are John William Graves, *Town and Country: Race Relations in an Urban-Rural Context, Arkansas 1865–1905* (Little Rock: University of Arkansas Press, 1990), 101; "Prominent Colored Citizens of Central Arkansas," *Biographical and Historical Memoirs of Pulaski, Jefferson, Ionoke, Faulkner, Grant, Perry, Garland and Hot Springs Counties, Arkansas* (Chicago: Goodspeed Publishing Co., 1889), 806 and 808; Fred Walter Dietrich, *The History of Dentistry in Arkansas: A Story of Progress* (Camden, Ark.: Arkansas State Dental Association, 1957) 45; and notecards of Florence Price Robinson (daughter of Florence B. Price), #40–43, located in the Price Materials, University of Arkansas.

Rae Linda Brown

Florence Irene Gulliver Smith, Price's mother, was a mulatto (an African American of mixed race) born in Indianapolis in 1854. Her father owned a chain of barbershops, and he and his wife invested in Indianapolis real estate. Growing up in an affluent household, she was given piano lessons and a good education. Florence taught elementary school, including music, for several years in Indianapolis. After she married Dr. Smith, ten years her senior, in November 1876, she resumed her teaching in Little Rock. The couple had three children: Charles (born October 1877, no known date of death), Florence Gertrude (born January 1880, died before age seven) and Florence Beatrice (1887–1953), the subject of this essay. At some point, Mrs. Smith left teaching to work as a secretary for the International Life and Trust Co. During this time she became a successful businesswoman, buying and selling Little Rock real estate in her own name.3

During the Reconstruction years (1865–77), a well-defined social structure of three distinct social classes developed within Little Rock's black community. This hierarchy comprised a complex web of characteristics that found expression among African Americans. The majority of blacks, at the base of the system, lived in poverty; they had little education and earned a living chiefly through manual labor. In the years after emancipation, many small entrepreneurial enterprises were developed, creating what amounted to a black middle class. The upper class, the smallest in number, included both old families and new. The two groups attained wealth in a variety of ways, including ownership of land businesses of every type, the professions of medicine and teaching, and work as blacksmiths and masons; they combined to form the nucleus of black Little Rock's political, economic, and sophisticated social base. Their behavior and attitudes "bore all the earmarks of gentility, super-respectability, and refinement."4

The "old families" were all former slaves born in or around the city. They included Rev. William Wallace Andrews, taught to read and write by his master, who founded Little Rock's first black public school. The other group within the black upper class, the "new families," comprised a handful of skilled and often well-educated blacks who settled in Little Rock from elsewhere following the Civil War. Dr. Smith was counted among this group.

In the late nineteenth century Little Rock was a bustling small city. Located on the Arkansas River, it had a population of about 38,000, seventy percent of which was white and thirty percent black. By 1900 the city could boast a thriving business section that included twenty-nine blacksmith shops, thirty-eight dry goods firms, several hotels, restaurants, and more than a hundred grocers. Just beyond the confines of the city, farms where cotton and sugar cane were grown were numerous. Crucial to the cotton industry were six railroad lines that fed into the city.5

Little Rock developed a self-sufficient black community. By the 1890s, blacks constituted fully one-third of Little Rock's population. In the decades since the Civil War, blacks had worked hard to buy land, earn livings, and educate their children. Domestics, skilled artisans, and black professionals, while not in the same social class, all contributed to the city's economic prosperity. Because of the opportunities for blacks, Little Rock became known as the South's "Negro Paradise." A survey taken in the 1890s shows that blacks owned eight wood and coal yards, ten blacksmith shops, two hotels, nine restaurants, two jewelry stores, a drugstore, a mortuary, a cemetery, a bank,

---

3. The information on Mrs. Smith's last years in Little Rock is gathered from the probate records of Dr. James H. Smith, Little Rock History Commission (state archives).

4. Willard B. Gatewood, "The Formative Years of William Grant Still: Little Rock, Arkansas, 1895–1911," in Catherine Parsons Smith, *William Grant Still: A Study in Contradictions* (Berkeley: University of California Press, 2000), 28.

5. John William Graves, *Town and Country: Race Relations in an Urban-Rural Context, Arkansas 1865–1905* (Little Rock: University of Arkansas Press, 1990), 101.

and several newspapers. There were fifteen cobblers and fifteen dressmakers, plus upholsterers and confectioners; among the city's professionals were fifty-five teachers, thirty-eight ministers, six lawyers, five physicians, and one dentist (Dr. James H. Smith).[6]

For all of the social attitudes associated with the black aristocracy, a central mission was individual and collective advancement of the race. Dr. Smith, who founded schools in rural Arkansas, was among many in his class who understood that only through education could the race be uplifted. For the privileged few, education meant Harvard or Yale, and for Florence Beatrice it meant the New England Conservatory of Music in Boston. Blacks who followed that path of education were all members of the upper class, and they returned to Little Rock to teach black children whose access to public school education was limited.

The Smiths were involved in many community affairs, and they socialized with black families who had similar interests. It was in Little Rock that Florence Beatrice met composer William Grant Still, who became a lifelong friend. Still's stepfather, Charles Shepperson, was a postal clerk, and Still's mother, Carrie (Still) Shepperson, was a teacher and community leader. Of the Smiths, Still said: "They belonged to our social set—which consisted of people who were interested in intellectual matters."[7] Carrie Shepperson was particularly active in bringing Negro artists to Little Rock. These artists included Clarence Cameron White (1880–1960), a noted composer and violinist who maintained a long friendship with Florence Beatrice, and E. Azalia Hackley (1867–1922), a singer and important promoter of Negro artists. Still's mother also organized the Lotus Club, a literary group first organized for women, that met regularly to discuss current events and debate political issues. Dr. Smith also led a literary club for men, each of whom brought books to be exchanged monthly.[8]

Florence Beatrice and William Grant Still (eight years her junior) attended the same schools. Charlotte Andrews Stephens first taught them at the Union School, which was both an elementary and high school. Though they were educated in a segregated school with facilities not equal to those of the white schools, both students received an excellent education from Mrs. Stephens, who had attended Oberlin College for two years. Her classroom was over-crowded as she tried to educate as many as ninety students each year. In 1902 the Union School was moved and its name changed to Capitol Hill. It was here that Florence Beatrice and Still completed high school. Carrie Still Shepperson taught in the high school's English department. Reflecting the city's lack of concern for the education of black children, the school had no library. Shepperson set about to rectify this by organizing an alumni group to put on benefit performances of Shakespeare plays. The resulting net of several hundred dollars was used to found the Capitol Hill library.[9]

From the beginning, the Smiths were included among the upper echelon in socially conscious Little Rock. Like most "aristocrats of color," they were mulattos; that is, they were of mixed racial heritage with fair complexions and Caucasian features. Their refined manners, cultural sophistication, and attractive outward appearance all contributed to their inclusion among the black elite and enhanced their acceptance by whites. For the Smiths, being light-skinned had brought with it certain privileges during the days of Reconstruction. There had been a certain amount of freedom to move

6. Graves, *Town and Country*, 117.

7. William Grant Still to Mary D. Hudgins, 3 February 1967. Mary Dengler Hudgins Research Files, folder 3, Price Materials, Mullins Library Special Collections, University of Arkansas. Also, William Grant Still, as told to Verna Arvey, "My Arkansas Boyhood," *Arkansas Historical Quarterly* 26/3 (Autumn 1967): 290; and Adolphine Fletcher Terry, *Charlotte Stephens: Little Rock's First Black Teacher* (Little Rock: Academic Press of Arkansas, 1973), 112.

8. D. B. Gaines, *Racial Possibilities as Indicated by the Negroes of Arkansas* (Little Rock: Philander Smith College, 1898).

9. Still, "My Arkansas Boyhood," 285–92.

Rae Linda Brown

about Little Rock unrestricted and to enjoy opportunities to advance economically. But when "Jim Crow" laws were instituted in the 1890s, all blacks, regardless of their social status, became second-class citizens through racist laws, which stripped them of their basic human rights.[10] By the time Florence Beatrice left for college in 1903, Little Rock was no more the "Negro Paradise" it had once been.

From 1903 to 1906 Florence Beatrice attended the New England Conservatory of Music in Boston. Although her studies at the Conservatory were concentrated in teaching and organ performance, she also became interested in composition. While a student at the Conservatory, Florence Beatrice wrote her first symphony and a string trio, both of them based on Negro folk music (neither of these scores has survived). She was enrolled in composition classes with Wallace Goodrich and Frederick Converse, two well-qualified teachers and composers. When she showed her symphony to George Whitefield Chadwick, however, the eminent composer offered Florence Beatrice a scholarship to study with him in his private studio. Chadwick's position as director of the New England Conservatory precluded him from teaching many students, but he accepted a few of the most gifted, giving them two-hour composition lessons and teaching some without pay.[11] In Chadwick, Florence Beatrice found a sympathetic teacher and perhaps even some inspiration. Several of Chadwick's compositions, including the Symphony no. 3 in F, his Quartet no. 4 in E Minor, and the symphonic ballad *Tam O'Shanter*, draw on vernacular sources, and Chadwick is acknowledged as a pioneer in writing concert music with an indigenous American flavor.[12]

Of the many hundreds of students who were admitted to the Conservatory with Florence Beatrice in 1903, only fifty-eight received degrees during the class commencement ceremonies in June 1906: thirty-one degrees were in piano performance, seven in organ performance, seven in vocal performance, four in violin performance, and nine in piano tuning training. Florence Beatrice, only nineteen years old, received two degrees—a Teachers Diploma in piano and a Soloists Diploma in organ, the highest attainable certificate awarded by the Conservatory. She completed the normally four-year degree programs in three years and was the only student that year to receive two degrees.

If Florence Beatrice had any serious career aspirations as a performer or as a composer at that time, she laid them aside after graduating from the Conservatory and returned home to teach. A sense of mission and service was deeply embedded in her, not only through her father's example of involvement in black social causes but by many members of the black community. Further, ties of family and tradition were

---

10. John William Graves, "Negro Disfranchisement in Arkansas," *Arkansas Historical Quarterly* 26 (Autumn 1967), 201.
11. Notecards of Florence Price Robinson, #44–54, Price Materials. This information was confirmed in the *Chicago Defender*, 4 May 1935, 7, and 11 July and 25 July 1936, 7. (John) Wallace Goodrich (b. 27 May 1871 in Newton, Mass.; d. 6 June 1952 in Boston) was an educator, conductor, and concert organist. He taught at the New England Conservatory for many years, becoming dean of the faculty in 1907 and succeeding Chadwick as director in 1931; he retired in 1942. Frederick Converse (b. 5 January 1871 in Newton, Mass.; d. 8 June 1940 in Westwood, Mass.) was a composer, teacher, and administrator. He taught harmony at the New England Conservatory from 1900 until 1902 and at Harvard from 1903 until 1907. From 1907–14 he was active as a composer, returning to the New England Conservatory in 1920. There he held many position until he retired in 1938. George Whitefield Chadwick (b. 13 November 1854 in Lowell, Mass.; d. 4 April 1931 in Boston) was a prominent American composer, educator, and conductor. As director of the New England Conservatory from 1897 until 1930, he developed the school's orchestra and much of its curriculum. His compositions show "Americanist" traits and reveal him to be a pioneer in this regard.
12. Steven Ledbetter and Victor Fell Yellin, "George Whitefield Chadwick," in *The New Grove Dictionary of American Music*, ed. by H. Wiley Hitchcock and Stanley Sadie (London and New York: Macmillan, 1986), I:385. Also Adrienne Fried Block, "Dvořák, Beach, and American Music," in *A Celebration of American Music: Words and Music in Honor of H. Wiley Hitchcock*, ed. Richard Crawford, R. Allen Lott, and Carol J. Oja (Ann Arbor: University of Michigan Press, 1990), 261–62.

strong. The expectation of her parents and of herself after college was to marry and to have a family. It would be many years before Florence Beatrice set pen to paper again to pursue her gifts as a composer.

Florence Beatrice's first teaching position was at the Cotton Plant-Arkadelphia Academy in Cotton Plant, Arkansas, about sixty-five miles from Little Rock. Supported by the white Presbyterian church, the small co-educational school for Negroes had a secondary school curriculum grounded in liberal arts. After less than a year at Cotton Plant, she began teaching at Shorter College in Argenta (North Little Rock) and held that appointment until 1910. Shorter College, one of Little Rock's three four-year, church-related colleges for black students, was founded and supported by the African Methodist Episcopal Church. Like many black colleges of that day, Cotton Plant and Shorter provided young students with an education that was an amalgam of elementary school, high school, and college.[13]

During the four years that Florence Beatrice taught in Arkansas, she lived at home with her parents. Dr. James Smith died on 10 April 1910 at the age of sixty-seven. The rather long obituaries in all the local papers list his many accomplishments, including the pioneering dental work he did in Chicago and Little Rock and his efforts as an artist, inventor, and author. A history buff and considered by some to be an authority on the Civil War, Dr. Smith was working on a second novel, *Black Mammies of the South*, at the time of his death.[14]

By now the South's rigid segregation laws were firmly in place, and Mrs. Smith, with no tolerance for injustice, was relegated to second-class citizenship together with all other blacks. This was not the life Mrs. Smith would live. With the help of attorney Thomas J. Price, her future son-in-law, she quickly settled her estate after the death of Dr. Smith. She sold everything she and her husband owned (including the cooking utensils!), effectively destroying all evidence of her life in Little Rock. Choosing to "pass" for white, Mrs. Smith returned to Indianapolis and "disappeared" to become part of the majority culture. No trace of her has been found after she left Little Rock in March 1911, less than a year after Dr. Smith's death.[15]

With her mother gone, Florence Beatrice left the city for Atlanta in September 1910, several months after her father died. There she accepted a position as Head of the Music Department at Clark University (now Clark Atlanta University). As department head (composer, artist-in-residence, and music teacher), Florence Beatrice coordinated all of the musical programs, including those of the students and guest artist concerts. She regularly gave organ and piano recitals and brought nationally and internationally recognized Negro artists to campus for concerts. Students heard performances of concert singers E. Azalia Hackley, Anita Patti Brown (ca. 1870–ca. 1950), and Florence Cole Talbert (1890–1961), concert violinists Joseph Douglass (1871–1935)

13. For general information on blacks in higher education, see Henry Allen Bullock, *A History of Negro Education in the South: from 1916 to the Present* (Cambridge: Harvard University Press, 1967). See also Bernice Lamb McSwain, "Shorter College: Its Early History," *Pulaski County Historical Review*, 30 (Winter 1982): 81–84. Price's employment from 1906–12, while on the faculty of Cotton Plant-Arkadelphia Academy, Shorter College, and Clark University, is not documented through school catalogs. Music was considered a supplement to the core education of these schools; faculty members are not listed, but Price's faculty appointments are documented in several sources. See Mildred Denby Green, *Black Women Composers: A Genesis* (Boston: G.K. Hall, 1983). Green interviewed Neumon Leighton, a friend of Price at Cotton Plant. Her teaching positions are discussed in a letter from Solar Carethers, piano teacher, to Mary D. Hudgins, 22 November 1967. Hudgins file, Price Materials, University of Arkansas. Price's positions were also noted in *Opportunity* 10 (December 1932), 391.

14. Dr. James H. Smith's obituary, with information about his current work projects, was carried in the *Arkansas Gazette* (17 April 1910) and the *Chicago Defender* (7 May 1910).

15. Florence Price Robinson, Florence Irene Gulliver Smith's granddaughter, wrote of Mrs. Smith's leaving Little Rock in her notecards (#40–43), which are included in the Price Materials, University of Arkansas.

and Clarence Cameron White, Carl Diton (1886–1962), the first Negro pianist to make a transcontinental tour, and Hazel Harrison (1883–1969), a pianist who became known internationally.[16]

The students at Clark University heard a variety of music, including arrangements of spirituals and instrumental music by such Negro composers as White, Diton, and Samuel Coleridge-Taylor. The guest artists, particularly the instrumentalists, who were excluded from most concert halls because of their race, also benefited, because Clark University provided them with opportunities to perform. The students lived vicariously through these artists who survived and thrived in spite of the difficulties they faced. As was the case at Clark University's sister institutions, the school choir traveled extensively, publicizing the school and popularizing Negro spirituals. Under Florence Beatrice's tutelage, the students at Clark University enthusiastically embraced the European music tradition as well as the music of Negro composers. As they developed their talents, their cultural awareness was extended from the campus into the community.

While she was in Atlanta, Florence Beatrice became friends with many professional musicians including Kemper Harreld (1885–1971), an established educator, accomplished pianist, and concert violinist. Harreld was brought to Atlanta in 1911 by President John Hope of Atlanta Baptist College (now Morehouse College) to establish a music department. At the college, Harreld organized an orchestra and string quartets, and he led the Glee Club to become a nationally respected ensemble. Florence Beatrice and Harreld maintained their friendship long after she left Atlanta. She occasionally saw him when his choir performed in Chicago, and they appear to have corresponded with each other through the 1940s.[17]

In 1912 Florence Beatrice returned to Little Rock to marry Thomas Jewell Price, a successful attorney whom she met while she was still teaching at Shorter College. (It was Thomas Price who had helped Mrs. Smith, Florence Beatrice's mother, to sell her household goods in March 1911 before she left for Indianapolis.)

Already a distinguished lawyer in Washington, D.C., Thomas Price had arrived in Little Rock in 1908.[18] He was born in New Haven, Connecticut, on 2 April 1884 to Eugene B. and Caroline Roberts Price.[19] After graduating from Hillhouse High School (1902), he left Connecticut for Howard University in Washington, D.C., from which he received his law degree in 1906. While attending Howard, Thomas Price began clerking for the distinguished black judge Robert H. Terrell (1857–1925).[20] After passing the bar exam, he earned a special certification to try cases in the U.S. Supreme Court and in the U.S. Circuit Court of Appeals in the 7th and 8th districts of

---

16. Price's appointment at Clark University was noted in *Opportunity* 10 (December 1932), 391. Also, her appointment and activities were verified in the following: correspondence to the author from Florence Crim Robinson, Fuller E. Callaway Professor of Music, Clark College, 5 November 1986; correspondence to the author from Doris Smith, administrative assistant to the President, Clark College, 21 October 1988; and a program announcement written by J. de Koven Killinsworth, Professor of Music, Clark College, 9 April 1972. For a fuller discussion of the history of Clark College see James P. Brawley, *Clark College Legacy: An Interpretive History of Relevant Education, 1869–1975* (Atlanta: Clark College, 1977). Brawley was Acting President of the College in 1940–41 and President in 1941–65. Information about the school was also gleaned from the Clark University catalogs, 1910–11.

17. Information on the relationship between Kemper Harreld and Price came from many personal conversations with his daughter, Josephine Harreld Love (1914–2003), throughout 1986.

18. Thomas Yenser, ed., *Who's Who in Colored America*, 4th ed. (1933–37), 5th ed. (1938–40), 6th ed. (1941–44) (Yonkers-on-Hudson, N.Y.: C. E. Burckel).

19. The birth certificate of Edith Price (daughter of Thomas and Florence Price), filed 2 April 1921, lists Price's date of birth as 1882 but the *Who's Who* volumes place Price's birth in 1884. Given the lengthy biographies in these volumes, I have chosen to place Price's birth date in 1884.

20. Judge Terrell's wife, Mary Church Terrell, was one of the foremost spokespersons for black women's rights, organizing the National Colored Women's League in 1892. In 1901 she became the first president of the National Association of Colored Women's Clubs in America.

Washington, D.C. In 1908 he moved to Little Rock to join the law firm of Scipio Africanus Jones, the city's most prominent black lawyer. From 1908 to 1921 Price and Jones were partners, establishing one of the most powerful and lucrative law firms in the city. Their office was located downtown at 402 W. Markham.[21] Price and Jones were involved in real estate as well; from 1908 to 1911 Price was a stockholder in Jones's Arkansas Realty and Investment Company.

During the summer of 1912 Florence Beatrice returned to Little Rock to marry this successful lawyer. They were married by a Justice of the Peace on 9 September 1912.[22] For a year the couple lived at 1904 Cross St.; in September 1913 they moved to a lovely home at 2417 Cross. The house was located near Dunbar High School in a middle-class, predominately black neighborhood. The Price neighbors were professionals; many of them taught at the high school.

After they married, Thomas and Florence Price probably never considered living anywhere other than Little Rock. Despite the existence of Jim Crow laws and race-based violence, Little Rock was still considered a good place to be for upwardly mobile blacks. Little Rock's black middle class, the "aristocrats of color," had changed little since its emergence in the late nineteenth century. Education, wealth, and respectability remained the foremost criteria for membership in this group. Willard Gatewood writes: "Because attendance or graduation from college by blacks, not to mention the acquisition of advanced degrees, was so rare, those who did have college diplomas enjoyed special distinction and were expected to assume leadership roles."[23] As in Reconstruction days, these citizens' cultural life centered on literary and musical activities, black institutions of higher learning, and the church.[24]

For black citizens of Little Rock, Ninth Street was the heart of the city. It was here that the offices of most blacks—physicians, lawyers, businessmen—could be found. Blacks ventured to Ninth Street to find everything from "medical services and spiritual nourishment to Saturday night entertainment." Referred to as "the Line," Ninth Street was the border between black and white Little Rock.[25] Mrs. Judith Finn, one of Price's former students, remembers the street this way:

> [It was] a busy, busy street on every corner. People who were shopping on Main Street, especially men, and people who came from the Rock Island Station in the East End would walk to Main Street and stay awhile. Then they would continue around the corner, Ninth and Main on down to . . . Ninth and Arch. And they would congregate there in groups and they would always have a lot of fun . . . . It was a nice and exciting place on Sundays. After church everybody was going to the drug store getting ice cream, sitting down. As I say, that's where you intermingled and met other children.
>
> One of the centers of activities along the Ninth St. corridor was the Mosaic Templars building. Many professional offices were located in the building, including many of the city's black doctors, and there was an auditorium where dances were held. In the 1930s all of the famed big jazz bands came to play there including Cab Calloway and Louis Armstrong.[26]

---

21. In addition to the *Who's Who* volumes, information on Price's career was gleaned from the Little Rock city directories, 1906–28. See also Tom W. Dillard, "Scipio A. Jones: Fought Mobs, Climbed Rungs of GOP Politics," *Arkansas Gazette*, 30 January 1979, 4B. Also, *The Messenger* 10/1 (January 1928), 10.

22. Little Rock History Commission, marriage licenses, book 53, 463.

23. Willard B. Gatewood, *Aristocrats of Color, The Black Elite, 1880–1920* (Bloomington: Indiana University Press, 1990), 265.

24. Earnest Lamb, "From Spiritual to Symphony: A Portrait of Florence Price." Radio broadcast transcript. Broadcast on KLRE and KUAR, Little Rock, 11 and 13 February 1993. In Price Materials, University of Arkansas.

25. Willard B. Gatewood, "The Formative Years of William Grant Still: Little Rock, Arkansas, 1895–1911," in *William Grant Still: A Study in Contradictions*, ed. Catherine Parsons Smith (Berkeley: University of California Press, 2000), 26.

26. Lamb interview, "From Spiritual to Symphony," 18–19.

Rae Linda Brown

By all accounts Florence Price and her husband were active in Little Rock's black community. In addition to teaching, Florence served as president and director of the Little Rock Club of Musicians, an organization that sponsored musical programs. Thomas Price was a much sought-after lawyer. In 1914 he was elected as an alternate delegate to the Pulaski County Negro Republican Convention, one of the two segregated political conventions (one for blacks and one for whites) held that year in Little Rock.[27] He was also legal advisor to several black organizations and fraternal groups, including the Supreme Royal Circle of Friends of the World (from 1917), the Knights of Pythias (1924–28), and two insurance companies (1918–28). Perhaps one of his most important positions was attorney to the Mosaic Templars, an international benevolent organization for Negroes, founded in Little Rock by John E. Bush and still headquartered there. Thomas Price was also a District Grand Secretary for the Odd Fellows and a Grand Chancellor for the Knights of Pythias.[28]

The Prices started a family soon after they were married. Their first-born child was a son, Thomas Jr., whom Florence Beatrice called Tommy. She immediately set her feelings to music in a poignant art song, "To my little son" (lyrics by author Julia Johnson Davis). Price uses romantic harmonies and a nostalgic text ("In your face I sometimes see shadowings of the man to be . . . in twenty years and one. . . . Then shall I, wistful try to trace the child you once were in your face") to evoke a mother's love for her son and the bond that exists between them. Tommy died, however, while very young. Although there is no date on the unpublished song, it appears to be one of Price's earliest works for voice.

The Prices had two other children. Their daughter Florence Louise was born 6 July 1917 and a second daughter, Edith Cassandra, was born 29 March 1921. After these children were born, Perry Quinney (later Johnston), a student at Arkansas Baptist College, moved in with the family to help take care of the girls. Having a caretaker for her children gave Florence Price time to teach, compose, and be active in outside musical activities. Perry Quinney and Price became the best of friends—their friendship was to last a lifetime.

When she married, Price abandoned her college teaching career and, like many women, stayed home to raise her children. However, she did establish a music studio and taught piano and violin lessons. Price became one of black Little Rock's most sought-after music teachers, with a reputation for giving her students solid backgrounds in piano technique and music theory (including regularly transposing music).[29] Rather than relying solely on the piano method books of others, Price wrote her own "studies" at beginning, intermediate, and advanced levels, each emphasizing a different aspect of piano technique. Many of these pieces have fanciful titles meant to appeal to the imagination of children. For example, "Brung, the bear" stresses the five-finger hand position and the use of the thumb on the black keys while "The froggie and the rabbit" is a study in rhythm. Other pieces introduce six-eight rhythm, shifts of hand positions, intervals, and exercises to strengthen fingers.

Price continued to work on her composing and soon began to receive outside monetary encouragement for her work. During the 1920s foundations began to support black composers and performers with awards and fellowships. The Rockefeller and Rosenwald Fellowships were primarily offered to performers, but in 1925 Casper Holstein, a black businessman from New York, began to offer prize money to composers through the black periodical *Opportunity*. Other important fellowships

---

27. *Arkansas Gazette*, 7 July 1914. I am grateful to Tom Dillard, former archivist, University of Central Arkansas, for sharing this information with me.

28. Thomas Price's activities are documented in *Who's Who in Colored America*, 4th ed. (1933–37), 5th ed. (1938–40), and 6th ed. (1941–44).

29. Lamb interviews with former students Mrs. Judith Finn and Mrs. Edith Flakes, "From Spiritual to Symphony."

established around this time included the Harmon Foundation Awards for composition and performance and the Rodman Wanamaker Composition Contest, established in 1927 and offering prizes in several categories: songs, choral works, symphonic works, and solo instrumental pieces.[30]

Price entered several of her small-scale piano compositions into these competitions. Using the southern landscape as her inspiration, she composed *In the Land o' Cotton* for piano, and this tied for second prize in *Opportunity* magazine's Holstein prize in May 1926. In 1927, she was again awarded second prize in the same contest for *Memories of Dixieland*, also for piano. In the same year her husband entered her piano piece *At the Cotton Gin, a Southern Sketch* in a composition contest, and Price won both a cash prize and the work's publication by G. Schirmer (1928.)[31]

Serious about improving her craft as a composer, Price spent the summers of 1926 and 1927 at the Chicago Musical College. There she studied composition with Carl Busch and Wesley La Violette and harmony and orchestration with the latter.[32] She did some additional work in composition with Arthur Olaf Anderson. And, perhaps contemplating the possible financial necessity of a career in public school music, she took a course in Public School Music Methods.[33]

Price's frequent trips to Chicago suggest that as early as 1926 Price anticipated leaving Little Rock. Financial difficulties in her home were a big problem. Though she earned a steady income from her private teaching, it appears that by the late 1920s her husband's law practice was not doing well. Her student, Mrs. Finn, reports:

> I saw Mr. Price in the home before he went to work in the mornings. He was a lawyer and . . . I was thinking also how softly she would speak to him about leaving home and going down to see about his work. 'Cause I had been in other peoples homes when their husbands and wives would [be] talking together [and] it was much harsher. But she said so sweetly what she said to him. And she was stern with that. She meant for him to get out there and find something to do. Lawyers weren't making money then.[34]

To make matters worse, the racial tension in Little Rock had become intolerable. The Negro newspapers repeatedly carried stories of racial atrocities, and lynching persisted even in middle class neighborhoods where the families of prominent blacks lived.[35] While Price lived in Little Rock, her way of life as a Negro woman, to some extent, had been determined for her. Social custom included an obligation to care for her parents, teach, marry, and raise her children. After the "Jim Crow" laws forced her to abdicate her rights, she continued to forge ahead on her career, although with increasing difficulty.[36]

---

30. Eileen Southern, *The Music of Black Americans: A History*, 2nd ed. (New York: Norton, 1983), 396. See also: *The Messenger* 9 (1927): 14.

31. *Opportunity* (May 1926), 157, and *Opportunity* (May 1927), 204–205, incl. photo. See also Notes of Florence Price Robinson, Price Materials, University of Arkansas.

32. Before arriving in Chicago, Busch (1862–1943) founded and conducted several regional orchestras, including the Kansas City Symphony (1911–18). He was a noted teacher of string instruments, theory and composition and from 1924–38 taught at several colleges and universities, including the Chicago Musical College. La Violette (1894–1978) began his eight-year tenure at the college, as composition teacher and ultimately dean, just after completing his doctorate in music there. Anderson (1880–1958), music educator, theorist, and composer, was head of the theory department and a member of the faculty from 1908–29.

33. Price's academic transcripts, Chicago Musical College, summer sessions 1926 and 1927. Price Materials, University of Arkansas.

34. Lamb interview, 17.

35. One of the most heinous incidents was the lynching of a black man in front of Bethel A.M.E. church in 1927. See "Mob Lawlessness: That Lynch-Murder and Burning at the Stake in Arkansas, Last Week, Inexcusable in a Civilized Country—Fear," *Cleveland Gazette*, 14 May 1927, 1. Price's family members confirmed with me that they had been threatened as well.

36. When Price applied to the Arkansas Music Teachers Association, for example, in spite of her impeccable academic and teaching credentials, she was denied admission because of her color. See Mildred Denby Green, *Black Women Composers: A Genesis* (Boston: G.K. Hall/Twayne Publishers, 1983), 32.

In 1927 Price and her family moved to Chicago in order to escape the oppressive social proscriptions of the South. By moving northward to Chicago, the Price family followed the path taken by thousands of Negroes from the turn of the century through the decades after World War I. For most Negroes the impetus behind this mass migration was economic. Chicago was considered by many to be a land of opportunity, and Negroes wanted to escape from a section of the country where freedom and equal opportunity were denied them. Chicago helped restore Price's artistic impulse. She discovered a city full of vitality and an environment that was conducive to her creative energy. Opportunities, both social and professional, were many. Conversations and collaborations with visual artists, dancers, writers, and actors harkened back to Price's childhood, when Little Rock was intellectually and culturally richer than it had lately become.

In 1919 Chicago hosted the National Convention of Musicians, from which was formed the National Association of Negro Musicians (NANM), an organization founded to promote black classical music and to support African-American composers and performers of concert music. Branches sprang up immediately throughout the country. The first branch was the Chicago Music Association, which held its meetings at the Wabash Avenue YMCA. In its early years, this group, whose first president was Nora Holt, music columnist for the *Chicago Defender* from 1917–23, gave scholarships to young, deserving musicians. The first scholarship was awarded to Marian Anderson, who appeared as soloist with the city's Umbrian Glee Club in 1919 while still a high school student. In 1922 a second Chicago branch of NANM formed, named for composer R. Nathaniel Dett. The R. Nathaniel Dett Club of Music and Allied Arts met at the National Conservatory of Music and had a membership of mostly younger and not yet well-established black musicians. Opera singer La Julia Rhea and concert organist Orrin Clayton Suthern II were members of the Dett Club who would establish themselves nationally.37

NANM was, arguably, the most important classical music organization for blacks from the 1920s on. In Chicago, the NANM branches sponsored musical programs that featured well-known musicians in recital, and they held lecture-performances for the benefit of both the black and white community. Their concerts also promoted the work of Chicago's African-American composers.

Although Price joined the R. Nathaniel Dett Club in April 1928, holding various offices including chair of the composition committee, she was equally active and became more visible through her activities in the Chicago Music Association. It was through this branch of NANM that Price met many distinguished members of the black community, including Maude Roberts George, music critic of the *Chicago Defender* in the 1920s and '30s; Estella Bonds, mother of composer Margaret Bonds, whose salon gatherings in the 1930s of musicians, writers, and artists became legendary; and concert singer Anita Patti Brown. Price was present at nearly every meeting of the Chicago Music Association. She gave talks on "current events," accompanied members of the club on the piano or organ, demonstrated and lectured on rare keyboard instruments at local museums, composed music for club members, performed her own organ and piano compositions, and represented the branch at national meetings of NANM. Price's activities were regularly covered by Maude Roberts George in her music column for the *Chicago Defender*. Indeed, during the 1930s, hardly a week went by without some mention of Price's performances in the local or national edition of this newspaper.

Price was active at the national meetings of NANM as well, and it was at these meetings that she connected with black musicians across the musical spectrum. At the

---

37. "Whispers of Love: A History of the R. Nathaniel Dett Club of Music and Allied Arts, 1922–1987." Unpublished typescript given to me by Helen White, Chicago, 1988.

1940 conference, for example, she was honored for her work as a composer, performer, and educator. W. C. Handy, who gave a talk on the effect of radio on sales of musical scores written by African Americans, was the other honoree. At this conference, seminars were held by composer Camille Nickerson, chair of the music department at Howard University, composer William Dawson, and violinist Kemper Harreld of the Morehouse College (Atlanta) music department, the outgoing President of NANM in 1940.

Once settled in Chicago, Price continued to write teaching pieces for children—primarily for piano, but also some for organ and for violin with piano accompaniment. Creating a niche for herself in this genre, she easily secured publishers and found these compositions to be a profitable endeavor. She established a long-term relationship with Chicago's McKinley Music Company, which began to publish her music from 1928. The firm published more than twenty-five of Price's compositions during her career. Other Chicago publishers of Price's teaching pieces include Gamble Hinged Music and Clayton F. Summy. In addition, Theodore Presser, Carl Fisher, and G. Schirmer published her teaching pieces as well as her concert works for piano.

Many of Price's intermediate level teaching pieces feature characteristic African-American dance rhythms, notably the juba. *Levee Dance* (Theodore Presser, 1937) and "Ticklin' Toes" from *Three Little Negro Dances* (Theodore Presser, 1933) are typical. Most unusual about many of these pieces is Price's use of 4/8 rhythm. This usually occurs when she is interested in highlighting the rhythmic intricacies of the African-American folk dance with its highly syncopated right hand and steady oom-pah pattern in the left hand. The juba dance would later find its way into many more of Price's compositions, including her concert piano works and orchestral music. For the advanced student there are many unpublished works. *Moon Behind a Cloud, Flame,* and *Placid Lake* have much in common with her larger-scale concert works such as *Dances in the Canebrakes* and the Sonata in E Minor, but they are much shorter (two to five pages, typically). Thick chords, varied rhythms alternating triplets and sixteenths in succession, arpeggios, many tempo and dynamic changes, rhythmic figures shared between the hands, and extended chromatic chordal passages are all common features.

Together with her teaching pieces and classical works for piano, organ, and various chamber ensembles, Price in Chicago wrote popular songs, sometimes under the pen name "Vee Jay." Some of her songs were sung in the theater, others were arranged for radio performances. Many of them set texts by Chicagoans: a group of love songs by Sal Janeway Carroll composed in 1930 including "Love Dreams," "In Back o' the Clouds," "Let's Build a Little Love Nest," and "What's the Use?"; settings by Grace Linley published in 1928 by the Linley Music House including "The Island Of My Dreams" and "You Didn't Know This Baby"; settings by Frank Blaha published in 1928 including "Won't You Please Play Santa Claus?" and "Just a Dream That Never Came True"; and a setting by Joseph R. Gregory published in 1928 titled "A Smiling Face: Fox Trot."[38]

In the late 1920s and early '30s, Price's compositional output was startlingly eclectic. In the manner of a musician seeking to make a living by writing music, she composed for a wide variety of venues. On the classical front, on both local and national levels she was one of the most visible members of NANM, a mainstay of artistic idealism. She held a variety of offices, and her music was championed and performed regularly by esteemed artists—including organist Orrin Clayton Suthern II and pianist-composer Margaret Bonds—who were associated with the organization. It was through NANM that Price met concert singer Marian Anderson, who had about fifty of Price's songs in

---

38. All of this music is lost, but information on copyrights may be found at the Library of Congress Copyright Office.

Rae Linda Brown

her collection and who performed the composer's songs around the world. Among her publishers in this realm are G. Schirmer, Theodore Presser, Handy Brothers Music Co., Edward B. Marks, and the organ publishers Lorenz and Galaxy.

Price's compositional output of popular music is large, and in this realm she worked with a different set of publishers that included Linley Music House. As already noted, too, she was most prolific in producing pedagogical works, which involved McKinley, Clayton F. Summy, Carl Fisher, and other publishers. Indeed, after moving to Chicago in 1927, Price explored all the professional avenues available to her as a composer and performer. Her highest aspiration was certainly to succeed in the concert hall. Nevertheless, as an improviser of some repute, she also navigated and thrived in popular music idioms. Other composers of the period, including George Gershwin, William Grant Still, and James P. Johnson—male composer-performers conversant with improvised oral traditions as well as the written tradition—are known for traversing the terrain between classical and popular music. As a female composer, Price stands unique among her contemporaries.

In addition to taking care of her family, teaching, composing, and engaging vigorously in outside musical activities, Florence Price found time to further her musical studies. Through the efforts of Charles J. Haake, a faculty member at the American Conservatory of Music, she won a scholarship to study orchestration there in 1929. Haake and his wife, Gail, were also editors of the Oxford Piano Course in which some of Price's music would later be published. During the 1930s, Price continued to expand her academic knowledge, studying at the Chicago Teachers College and at the University of Chicago, where she pursued long-time interests in the liberal arts and in foreign languages.[39]

The 1929 stock market crash drew America into the economic hardship of the Great Depression. Jobs were hard to come by, even for lawyers. It appears that Thomas Price went for long stretches without work, and the financial strain of a home with no primary wage earner pushed Thomas and Florence to their limits. The Price family was soon in dire financial straits. Desperate, Florence Price became innovative in her efforts to earn money. Drawing on her skill as an improviser, which she may have acquired in Boston, she became adept at accompanying silent films on the organ in movie theaters.[40] Most of these theaters were located on "The Stroll," also known as the "Broadway of the Black Belt," an area that featured fifteen vaudeville and movie houses. Each of these venues hired pianists and organists to play for the stage productions and silent films.[41] Some of this music was improvised, but most of it was scored.

Price was one of the few women organists working along The Stroll, and she proved she had the required skills. This versatility was not unusual for many of Chicago's black classical and jazz musicians. Playing a variety of styles and being able to read music

---

39. *Opportunity* 10 (December 1932), 391.

40. My interview with Helen White, Chicago, 13 September 1988.

41. Though by the early 1930s most theaters exhibited sound films, some theaters continued to show silent films, and other theaters hired organists to play for entertainment. For example, Chicago theaters owned by Balaban & Katz (B & K) always offered live stage shows as well as movies. Douglas Gomery writes: "B & K so carefully nurtured local talent that, by the middle 1920s, it had become more famous for its impressive stage attractions, orchestras, and organists than for the movies. Shows celebrated fads and heroes, from Lindbergh to the Charleston to 'Jazz and Opera' week." Douglas Gomery, "Movie Palaces," *The Electronic Encyclopedia of Chicago* (Chicago: Chicago Historical Society, 2005). Available at http://www.encyclopedia.chicagohistory.org/pages/850.html.

"The Stroll" was the name given to State Street, in Chicago, between 26th and 39th Streets. From 1910 until the late 1920s it was the center of activity in the African-American community. In the evening, the street was active with people attending the jazz clubs; during the day, it was a popular area in which people congregated. See Shane White, "The Stroll," *Electronic Encyclopedia of Chicago* (Chicago: Chicago Historical Society, 2005). Available at http://www.encyclopedia.chicagohistory.org/pages/121.html.

were keys to survival, especially during the Depression. One jazz musician, William Everett Samuels, remembers the situation this way:

> The Black musicians who played classical music hung on. They survived the thirties. They were working in the theaters. They could always play, people like Dave Payton [sic] and Erskine Tate, and Jimmy Bell, Walter Dyett. They were all playing. They were all playing classical music because they had to play it in the theaters all the time. You see, all that stuff was scored [playing along with the silent movies] and they had to read the music. Much of it was classical. Blacks came out to hear it and see the movies. That's right. It wasn't that they liked the classics. It was not necessarily middle class Blacks that came to see the movies—it was all kinds. It was everybody. If you went to see the picture, you would have to hear the music. . . . Some go to see the pictures; some go to hear the music going with it. They just took it all in the package. You got a dose of culture.[42]

Lacking a steady job and feeling frustrated, Thomas Price saw his relationship with Florence Beatrice change. He was often angry and became abusive to his wife. In March 1930 he moved out of the family's residence, and a few months later Florence Beatrice began divorce proceedings. On 19 January 1931 Florence Price was granted a divorce and the custody of her two daughters.[43]

O Sing A New Song (1933–53)

During the mid-1930s Price composed several large-scale works, a remarkable achievement given the stress of her failed marriage and the need to support herself and her daughters. She was nothing if not creative, fiercely independent, and determined. It was with her Symphony in E Minor (1932), the Symphony in C Minor (1940), and the Piano Concerto in One Movement (1934) that she earned national recognition. The Symphony in E Minor was premiered by the Chicago Symphony Orchestra under the direction of Frederick Stock. Its performance—reviewed and acclaimed in the local press that included the *Chicago Defender*, the *Chicago Herald & Examiner*, and the *Chicago Daily News*—took place on 15 June 1933 at the "Century of Progress Exhibition" of the World's Fair. The Symphony in C minor was premiered at the Detroit Institute of Arts on 6 November 1940 by the Michigan WPA Symphony Orchestra under the direction of Valter Poole.[44] Both symphonies are treated in detail later in this essay.

In October 1933 Price began working on her Piano Concerto in One Movement. With the encouragement of Frederick Stock, she honed her orchestrating skills by attending rehearsals of the Chicago Symphony.[45] The Concerto was first performed, with Price at the piano, on 24 June 1934 in Orchestra Hall. The occasion was the sixty-seventh commencement exercise of the Chicago Musical College, where Price was taking graduate courses in composition and orchestration. Price played her concerto again

---

42. Donald Spivey, *Union and the Black Musicians: The Narrative of William Everett Samuels and Chicago Local 208* (Landam, Md.: University Press of America, 1984), 100.

43. Information on Florence Price's divorce is found in a transcript of the divorce proceedings, Circuit (Superior) Court of Cook Country, Chicago, 26 August 1930–19 January 1931.

44. On this concert, Poole also programmed Price's Piano Concerto in One Movement which featured the composer as soloist. Poole programmed the Symphony no. 3 again, two days later, on 8 November 1940. The latter concert included Johann Strauss's *Tales from the Vienna Woods* and George Enesco's *First Rumanian Rhapsody*. The programs of the Michigan WPA Orchestra are housed in the Detroit Public Library.

45. Price kept a diary during the 1930s but only a few pages of it remain. The information on Price attending Chicago Symphony rehearsals at Stock's invitation is noted in the entries for 5 December 1933 and 7 December 1933. There is also a letter to Price from Eric DeLamarter, assistant conductor of the Chicago Symphony, dated 6 February 1934, confirming that Stock would look at her newly composed Piano Concerto. Price Materials, University of Arkansas.

two months later, in a two-piano version, at the national convention of the National Association of Negro Musicians (NANM) in Pittsburgh, with Margaret Bonds playing the reduction of the orchestral accompaniment. The concerto received critical acclaim from reviewers in the local press. J. Fred Lissfelt of the *Pittsburgh Sun Press* noted Price's evolving style—a style that for him revealed a characteristic racial voice all her own. He wrote that "Florence Price's contribution in the form of a piano concerto was by far the most important feature of the concert for here we see what the Negro has taken from his own idiom and with good technique is beginning to develop alone. There is real American music and Mrs. Price is speaking a language she knows." After describing the formal structure of the concerto, Ralph Lewando of the *Pittsburgh Press* added, "coherent musical ideas prevail throughout, and the thematic material is logically developed."[46]

Just before the NANM performance, the Concerto was performed in Chicago at the Century of Progress Exhibition's Negro pageant, "O Sing a New Song." For this event, Price conducted a free-lance orchestra with Margaret Bonds at the piano. The pageant was a celebration of black music, dance, and drama from African origins through the 1920s. A "who's who" of black arts participated in the event, including bandleader and Broadway librettist-lyricist Noble Sissle, who organized the event and whose band played a medley of hits from his successful Broadway shows; composers N. Clark Smith, Harry Lawrence Freeman, Will Vodery, J. Rosamond Johnson, and Will Marion Cook; singer Abbie Mitchell; actor Richard B. Harrison; jazz pianist Earl Hines; and tap dance great Bill Robinson. The pageant concluded with the "story of the St. Louis Blues" conducted by W. C. Handy, composer of "The St. Louis Blues" (1914).[47]

Price's Piano Concerto in One Movement received more-than-local recognition on 12 October 1934 when the work was performed by the Woman's Symphony Orchestra of Chicago under the direction of Ebba Sundstrom at the Ford Symphony Gardens, part of the Century of Progress Exhibition. Margaret Bonds, who had played the concerto twice before, was the soloist. The Woman's Symphony Orchestra of Chicago, with 100 players, became probably the best known of the nation's women orchestras because of its regular concert season and radio broadcasts.[48] The 12 October program, devoted to women composers, was divided into two concerts: one in the afternoon and the other in the evening. Both were broadcast on WBBM-CBS radio. Before the concerts composer Carrie Jacobs-Bond delivered an address on "Women in Music." Mrs. H. H. A. Beach (Amy Beach), arguably America's most distinguished woman composer, whose *Gaelic Symphony* was also being performed that day, was honored as well.[49]

Price's concerto is extant in two manuscripts. One manuscript is an arrangement of the concerto for solo piano and orchestra reduction (for piano); another is an arrangement for two pianos. Using the extant instrumental parts and the orchestra reduction, it is possible to reconstruct the forces used to perform the work: two flutes, two oboes,

---

46. J. Fred Lissfelt, *Pittsburgh Sun Telegraph*, 31 August 1934, 27. Ralph Lewando, *Pittsburgh Press*, 31 August 1934, 27.

47. National Auditions Annual: A Century of Progress Souvenir Edition of Afro-American Pageant, Inc., Soldier Field, Chicago, 25 August 1934. Although Price may have conducted other orchestral works of her own during her career, this is the only documented occasion of her doing so.

48. See "Brief History of the Woman's Symphony Orchestra of Chicago," in Women's Symphony Orchestra Programs, Chicago Public Library, 1936–1940 (Chicago: n.p., n.d.). For more information on this orchestra and its activities see Linda Dempf, "The Woman's Symphony Orchestra of Chicago," *Notes* 62/4 (June 2006): 857–903.

49. See the programs of the 12 October 1934 concert, Chicago Public Library. See also: Eleanor Everest Freer, "Discrimination Against American Music," *Musical Leader* 66/26 (13 October 1934): 22. Glenn Dillard Gunn reviewed the performance and commented on Carrie Jacobs-Bond's talk in the *Chicago Herald and Examiner* (12 October 1934).

two bassoons, four horns, two trumpets, two trombones, strings, and percussion. As in many of Price's large-scale works, the concerto, in D minor, embraces aspects of the romantic tradition in orchestral music (among them, lush orchestration, colorful harmonies, and lyrical themes), but it also embodies many melodic, rhythmic, and harmonic aspects of African-American music. Though the work is titled a "Concerto in One Movement," it is divided into three distinct sections, modeling a conventional tempo arrangement of fast-slow-fast. Yet the three sections defy conventional forms. The first section, in a modified sonata-allegro form (its two contrasting themes are presented in complementary keys), is built around a spiritual-like theme unfolding over fifty-four measures; the second section offers the familiar call-and-response technique of many African-American folk melodies; the third section, a modified rondo (with a recurring theme that alternates with contrasting material), is based on the rhythms of the juba dance.[50]

Price wrote other orchestral works in the 1930s. Her Symphony no. 2 in G Minor is lost except for a single page at the Moorland-Spingarn Research Center at Howard University.[51] Another work, *Mississippi River (The river and the songs of those dwelling upon its banks)*, is a one-movement suite based on Negro folk themes. There is no evidence that either the symphony or the suite was ever performed. *Mississippi River* was completed in 1934 and dedicated to Price's teacher Arthur Olaf Anderson. The work requires the normal complement of strings, winds, and brass, along with percussion augmented by an Indian drum and a marimba. *Mississippi River* is one of the few Price works in which literal quotations of folk music constitute the core of the work. No fewer than six full-fledged themes are included. Four of them are spirituals ("Nobody Knows the Trouble I've seen," "Stand Still Jordan," "Deep River," and "Go Down Moses") and the other two (the "Steamboat Bill River Song" and a tune Price calls "Lalotte") are secular, upbeat themes.

The years 1933 to 1940 were very productive for Price. The period is marked by many performances of her piano, organ, vocal and orchestral music. Among the most popular of her compositions are two large-scale piano works, the Sonata in E Minor and *Dances in the Canebrakes*.[52] The three-movement sonata, which is rather conservative harmonically and structurally, is an expansive work in the romantic tradition. The first movement follows classic formal design. That is, the first movement is in sonata form (with two contrasting themes) and a slow introduction. The tender Andante second movement is in rondo form; once again, the recurring theme is a lyrical spiritual-like melody with characteristic syncopated rhythms and simple harmony. The sonata ends with a virtuosic scherzo-allegro movement; the movement's first section is based on a descending E minor scale, and the second section is infused with syncopated dance rhythms that Price found particularly expressive of her African-American roots. As for *Dances in the Canebrakes*, "based on authentic Negro rhythms," it is a suite in three movements, each with a fanciful title. "Nimble Feet" is a lively dance characterized by a dotted-rhythm melody in the bass. "Tropical Noon" is more introspective. "Silk Hat and Walking Cane" aspires to capture the grace and spirit of the cakewalk, a favorite antebellum dance. The descriptive title refers to the fine attire slaves wore during the dance as they pranced around in high-step, each couple hoping to win the coveted prize cake.

---

50. For a full discussion of Price's Piano Concerto in One Movement see the author's article, "The Woman's Symphony Orchestra of Chicago and Florence B. Price's Piano Concerto in One Movement," *American Music* 11/ 2 (Summer 1993): 185–205.

51. The Symphony no. 2 in G Minor is dated 193- on the first page.

52. Price's Piano Sonata in E Minor was completed in 1932. I edited the Sonata, which was published by G. Schirmer in 1997. *Dances in the Canebrakes* was published posthumously in 1953 by Affiliated Musicians/Mills Music. Documented performances of the work confirm that it was composed in 1933. See Maude Roberts George, "Music News," *Chicago Defender*, 24 June 1933, 15.

Rae Linda Brown

Throughout 1933 and 1934 Price remained visible at the Century of Progress Exhibition. She was a regular guest—as solo pianist, piano accompanist for singers performing her music, and lecturer—at the composer-artist programs sponsored by the National Council of Women. Price also had a program of her music presented by the Illinois Host House. It was at one of these concerts that she met Carrie Jacobs-Bond, probably America's most successful female songwriter of the time. Thereafter, the music of these two women composers often appeared on the same Chicago concerts. With the activities of the Fair continuing in full swing, Price also had many opportunities to hear her choral music. She directed the Treble Clef [Glee] Club that often performed at the Fair at the invitation of James A. Mundy, who organized programs of African-American folk music and guest artists three times a week for the mixed black and white audiences. Price also composed numerous choral works during this time for performance by her own glee club and for the Florence B. Price A Cappella Chorus, directed by Grace W. Tomkins. The choir was organized in January 1933 and, although an amateur group, steadily received praise for its programs, often performing to large audiences throughout the city.53

By the mid-1930s Price's career was going strong but her personal life floundered. After divorcing Thomas Price, she married Pusey Arnett, thirteen years her senior, on 14 February 1931. That marriage failed, however, and after three years the couple separated.54 For a while, with no place of her own to live, Price and her daughters moved from one friend's home to another. Temporarily she lived at the home of T. Theodore Taylor, pianist-organist of her church, Grace Presbyterian. She also lived for a while at the home of Estelle Bonds. Although conditions there were crowded—in addition to Price and her daughters, singers Helen and Louis White also lived with the Bonds family—there were some advantages for Price.55 Bonds was a pillar of the black community. Artists, musicians, poets, writers, and dancers, all committed to supporting one another, frequented her home. The Bonds residence was often the venue for informal concerts by Chicagoans and black artists passing through town. Others came by just to share the company. Margaret Bonds said: "From my mother, I had actual physical contact with all living composers of African descent." She added: "My mother had a collector's nose for anything that was artistic, and, a true woman of God, she lived the Sermon on the Mount. Her loaves and fish fed a multitude of pianists, singers, violinists and composers, and those who were not in need of material food came for spiritual food. Under her wings many a musician trusted."56 It was at Bonds's home

---

53. The information on Price's activities from summer 1933 to early 1934 is taken from Maude Roberts George, "Music News," *Chicago Defender*, 8 July 1933, 15; 15 July 1933, 15; 29 July 1933, 15; 12 August 1933, 15; 9 September 1933, 15; 30 September 1933, 15; 7 October 1933, 6; 28 October 1933, 12; 5 November 1933, 12; 11 November 1933, 12; and 20 January 1934, 12.

54. One month after her divorce from Thomas Price, Florence, at age 42, married Pusey Arnett, age 55, on Valentine's Day, 1931. Florence Price did not change her name, though on occasion she did use the name Price-Arnett. The information on Price's marriage to Arnett is taken from their marriage license (dated 11 February 1931) and marriage certificate (dated 14 February 1931). Cook County Clerk, Office of Vital Records, Chicago. By tracking Florence Price's addresses in phone directories and on copyright records, it appears that she and Arnett were separated by 1934 and that she and her daughters had moved out of her second husband's home. Since Price and Arnett did not divorce, there are no records that reveal the cause of the separation. Pusey Dell Arnett died in Chicago on 8 July 1957 at the age of 81. His death certificate states that he was "widowed," implying that he and Florence Price never divorced. Medical Certificate of Death, Bureau of Statistics, Illinois Department of Public Health.

55. Price met Louis and Helen White through the Dett Club. When Louis was hired by WGN radio in 1930 to sing on Sunday mornings with the WGN radio symphony orchestra, he hired Price to orchestrate music for his broadcast performances. Information from the author's interviews with Helen White in 1986.

56. Margaret Bonds, "A Reminiscence" in *International Library of Negro Life and History: The Negro in Music and Art*, compiled and edited by Lindsay Patterson under the auspices of the Association for the Study of Negro Life and History (New York: Publishers Co., 1967), 192.

that Price met many distinguished black artists including sculptor Richmond Barthé and poets Countee Cullen and Langston Hughes.[57] It was at this time that Price became especially close to Margaret Bonds and began to oversee her increasing interest in composition.

Once Price was able to re-establish herself on her own, she began again to accept invitations to perform. Although she preferred to spend her time composing, she did occasionally play recitals, most of them associated with the National Association of Negro Musicians or the church musicales. Late in 1934 she received an especially intriguing invitation. Would she consider returning to Little Rock to play a benefit piano recital at Dunbar High School? The concert, to be sponsored by the Philander Smith College Alumni Association, would be held on 19 February 1935. Price was not eager to return to the South, whose system of institutionalized racism, while marching under the banner of "separate but equal" for public school systems, fell far short of achieving such equality.[58] Dunbar High, however, was the successor to the Union School, her alma mater. Hoping to return something to the community that had nurtured her, Price accepted the invitation.

The alumni of Little Rock's black high school were proud of Price, for here black people could witness the success of one of their own. Advertisement for the concert was placed in several newspapers including the *Arkansas Democrat*. The notice read:

> Florence B. Price who twice won the Wanamaker music prize in 1931 and 1932, will be presented in a piano recital at the Dunbar High School auditorium at 8 Tuesday evening. She is the only woman member of her race who has composed and written a symphony. Her prize winning "Symphony in E Minor" was played during the Century of Progress Exhibition in Chicago, by the Chicago Symphony Orchestra. She is a member of the Chicago Woman's Organist Association. Special reserved seats have been arranged for white persons. Price of admission will be 25 cents for adults and 15 for students and 50 cents for reserved seats. In her recital Tuesday evening, she will play only her own compositions.[59]

By all accounts, the concert was a success. The *Arkansas Survey-Journal* reported: "Mrs. Florence B. Price, noted musician of Chicago, thrilled a magnificent audience of eager listeners at the Auditorium, Tuesday night, February 19, where she appeared in recital. All of Little Rock turned out to hear her, and sat spell-bound throughout the entire performance."[60] The irony in the situation need hardly be pointed out: Price, a black pianist playing at a black school, sponsored by a black organization, appearing before an audience in which the white members received preferential treatment (reserved seating), a legally sanctioned protocol in the South in 1935. No matter, Price's return home was a success. She is said to have played well, and she helped to raise funds to support the Dunbar school, much as Carrie Still Shepperson (William Grant Still's mother) and other caring members of the black community had done for the Union and Capitol Hill schools that Price had attended in Little Rock as a child.

When Price returned to Chicago she shifted her attention from the piano to the organ. In March 1935 she became a member of the Chicago Club of Women Organists, the first African-American woman to do so. This organization gave Price the opportunity to perform her large-scale concert works for organ, including the Passacaglia and Fugue (1936), the Sonata no. 1 (1927), and the Suite no. 1 (1942). These works, in addition to the teaching pieces and the church music, reveal how accomplished Price was as an organist. In the last movement of the Suite, for example, the organist must execute sixteenth-note arpeggios alternating on three manuals and

57. Green, *Black Women Composers*, 47.

58. Little Rock High, built in 1927, cost $1.5 million; Dunbar was built at a cost of just $400,000 in 1928. Little Rock High's library had 11,000 volumes in 1927 while Dunbar's library had 5,000 in 1930.

59. *Arkansas Democrat*, 17 February 1935, 6.

60. *Arkansas Survey-Journal* (19 February 1935). Hudgins File, Price Materials, University of Arkansas.

Rae Linda Brown

sixteenth notes divided between the hands. These passages, inspired by late Baroque organ literature, recall passages of Bach's famous Toccata and Fugue in D minor. The lengthy coda in this work harkens to late nineteenth-century writing for the organ with its bravura five-note chords in each hand punctuated by octave pedals and chromatic manual scale passages.

By the mid-1930s Price had developed into a serious composer whose skills were no doubt strengthened and accelerated by the many opportunities she had to hear her music performed, particularly her songs, which were sung by professional artists as well as local singers. Price's art songs and arrangements of spirituals were among Marian Anderson's favorites. The diva's collection included more than fifty of Price's songs, many of which were dedicated to and sung by her.[61] The spiritual arrangement, "My Soul's been Anchored in de Lord," published by Gamble Hinged Music in 1937, gained wide recognition when Anderson used it to close her historic Lincoln Memorial concert in 1939. Anderson also performed the spiritual on 14 September 1942 on the nationally broadcast "The Bell Telephone Hour," a half-hour radio program of commercially sponsored music (both classical and popular) featuring a full orchestra conducted by Donald Voorhees. Voorhees arranged much of the program's music, and sometimes he hired arrangers such as William Grant Still; on this occasion, however, the arrangement for solo voice and orchestra was Price's own. That "My Soul's been Anchored in de Lord" was a favorite of Anderson is evident in that she continued to sing it around the world, including on her 1957 Russian concert tour during which she used it to close a group of spirituals.[62] Anderson's rendition of "Songs to the Dark Virgin" scored a similar success for the composer. Set to a Langston Hughes text, the art song was highly acclaimed by Eugene Stinson, critic for the *Chicago Daily News*, who wrote: " 'Songs to the Dark Virgin' as Miss Anderson (Marian) sang it, [was] one of the greatest immediate successes ever won by an American song."[63]

Price was successful professionally for many reasons, not the least of which was the supportive network she established shortly after her arrival in Chicago. The importance of women's musical groups in the 1930s and 1940s figure prominently. She was the first black member of the Chicago Club of Women Organists and the Musicians Club of Women, both clubs that supported women in their struggle to gain hard-earned recognition in the professional music fields, including that of composer. Both of these organizations regularly programmed Price's organ, piano, vocal, and choral compositions. Sometimes Price performed her own piano or organ music. For example, at a Chicago Club of Women Organists program on 19 November 1936, Price performed her Passacaglia and Fugue, the popular piece "Dainty Lass," and an arrangement of the spiritual "Steal Away." In all, twenty organ works written by Price survive. Teaching pieces, church music, and concert works are all represented.

Price became the first woman of color invited to join the Illinois Federation of Music Clubs and the Musicians Club of Women. As with the Chicago Club of Women Organists, the Musicians Club of Women was equally responsive to Price and promoted much of her music. In one concert, on 11 February 1947, members performed the Piano Concerto in One Movement (two-piano version) and several art songs, and the club's Lyric Ensemble performed a choral work. In another concert, on 8 February 1949, Price's *Suite for Brasses* (two trumpets, two horns, two trombones, tuba, and piano) was premiered.

---

61. The Marian Anderson Collection is housed at the Annenberg Rare Book and Manuscript Library, University of Pennsylvania.

62. "My Soul's been Anchored in de Lord" was first recorded by Marian Anderson (Victor LSC 2592). It was also recorded by Ellabelle Davis (London LPS-182 and Victor 1799) and by Leontyne Price (VIC–S VCS 7083 Victor). The orchestral arrangement remains unpublished.

63. Reprinted in the *Musical Courier*, 1 December 1952. *Songs to the Dark Virgin* was published by G. Schirmer in 1941.

Price was also the first African-American composer to be represented on music programs of the Illinois Federation of Music Clubs. Her relationship with this group came about when Gail and Martin Haake, editors of the Oxford Method series in which many of Price's teaching pieces were published, introduced Price to Anamay Owens Wales, a member of the Chicago Club of Women Organists and the Federation of Music Clubs. Wales would later report that members were still performing Price's music in 1974, more than twenty years after Price's death; in particular, she noted a performance that took place at a meeting of the group in Fargo, North Dakota, when the Orchestra of the International Peace Gardens performed two works "not printed on the program."[64]

Issues of gender, class, and race were ever present for black women in the first half of the century and the inherent conflicts faced by professional women were difficult to reconcile. For this reason, Price maintained an active involvement in the National Association of Negro Musicians (NANM). It was through NANM, and by extension, through the *Chicago Defender*—the city's black-owned newspaper, which covered the activities of the black community both locally and nationally—that Price's name was kept before the public for the twenty-five years she resided in Chicago.

Despite her rising recognition, Price struggled with a lack of self-confidence in her career. In a 1936 *Chicago Defender* interview, headlined "Keep Ideals in Front of You, They Will Lead to Victory, says Mrs. Florence B. Price," the composer was asked if she was satisfied with her work. Price responded:

> I feel deeply thankful for progress, but satisfaction—no, not satisfaction. I am never quite satisfied with what I write. I don't think creators ever are quite satisfied with their work. You see there is always an ideal toward which we strive, and ideals, as you know, are elusive. Being of spiritual essence they escape our human hands, but lead us on, and I trust upward, in a search that ends. I believe, only at the feet of God, the One Creator, and source of all inspiration.[65]

The consciousness that Price articulates here is, in many ways, about female socialization. Many women, particularly those from an upbringing such as Price's, hoped to be recognized for their accomplishments, yet they lacked the confidence to promote themselves actively.[66] Price herself wrote about this trait in letters to her friends and other professional associates. In personal notes attached to a press release for the first performance of her Symphony no. 3 in 1940, she wrote: "I was recalled to the stage again and again. Finally the women of the audience (White, I saw almost no colored faces at all) rose to their feet followed by the entire audience. I suppose that is something I should have publicized. However I am poor in pushing publicity when it comes to myself."[67] Self-assurance and aggressiveness, personality traits often associated with men, are important to success in many professions, particularly if one is outside the

---

64. Letter from Anamay Owen Wales to Barbara Garvey Jackson, 17 October 1974. Price Materials, University of Arkansas.

65. Goldie M. Walden, "Keep Ideals in Front of You: They Will Lead to Victory, Says Mrs. Florence B. Price," *Chicago Defender*, 11 July 1936, 7.

66. Gloria T. Hull, *Color, Sex, and Poetry* (Bloomington: Indiana University Press, 1987), 12. After Price was accepted for membership in the National Association for American Composers and Conductors, her daughter wrote to Claude Barnett, founder of the Associated Negro Press, on 4 March 1940, to ask him to promote her mother's achievement. She wrote: "Because mother is so reticent about mentioning her own achievements and because she feels that she is imposing on your good nature to give you such facts 'so often' as she puts it, I decided I would take it upon myself to tell you . . . I feel sure that you, like others who know mother personally know that she is really too modest for her own good." Florence Price to Claude A. Barnett, 4 March 1940. TS. 1p. Claude Barnett Papers, Chicago Historical Society.

67. It is unclear to whom this note was written. She goes on to talk about being brought to Atlanta for a recital; thus I speculate that the note was to her friend Kemper Harreld, who taught at Morehouse College until 1951 and at Spelman College until 1952. Personal notes included with the press materials for the Symphony no. 3. Price Materials.

Rae Linda Brown

realm of an established network—that is, a system of access to people who are in positions of power—where contacts can be easily made.

During her career Price recognized the polemics surrounding the female composer. In Judith Tick's article, "Passed Away Is the Piano Girl," the author outlines traits of women composers, drawn from Goethe's concept of womanhood, that were defined through sexual stereotypes. Femininity in music was purported to be delicate, sensitive, graceful, refined, and more lyrical, while masculinity in music was defined as powerful, noble, and more intellectual. Songs and piano pieces constituted the core of a woman composer's oeuvre while symphonies, opera, and chamber music remained the domain of men.[68]

On the one hand, Price did not subscribe to the characterization of her music as inherently feminine; on the other hand, she admitted being shy and less aggressive than necessary to pursue and sustain a high-powered career as a composer. For some time she suppressed her desires to be a successful nationally known composer of large-scale works, content to care for her family and reap local acclaim as a composer of piano music, songs, and piano teaching pieces. Her orchestral music was being performed by respected musical institutions—the Chicago Symphony, the Chicago Woman's Orchestra, and several local symphonic bands—and by numerous concert singers. Yet Price's ultimate goal was recognition of her large-scale works—symphonies, concertos, and symphonic overtures—by the old-guard East Coast musical establishment: the orchestras of Boston, New York, and Philadelphia. A performance of her music by one of these orchestras would ensure her place in the annals of music history. But this was not to happen in her lifetime.

Florence Price, like any woman composer of her generation, knew that the musical world viewed her work through a filter of stereotypes. She also knew that, in a concert life where the musical supply far outstripped demand, it was up to her to promote her music—especially the larger works, which would only be performed if those who controlled concert programming could be convinced that it was in their interest to perform them. Thus, beginning in 1935, Price wrote Serge Koussevitzky, conductor of the Boston Symphony, to argue the case for her symphonies. Koussevitzky was known for his enthusiastic support of American composers; not only did he perform American works but he commissioned new ones as well. Price's letter of 5 July 1943 was one of the longer ones:

> My dear Dr. Koussevitzky,
> To begin with I have two handicaps—those of sex and race. I am a woman; and I have some Negro blood in my veins.
> Knowing the worst, then, would you be good enough to hold in check the possible inclination to regard a woman's composition as long on emotionalism but short on virility and thought content;—until you shall have examined some of my work?
> As to the handicap of race, may I relieve you by saying that I neither expect nor ask any concession on that score. I should like to be judged on merit alone—the great trouble having been to get conductors, who know nothing of my work (I am practically unknown in the East, except perhaps as the composer of two songs, one or the other or which Marian Anderson includes on most of her programs) to even consent to examine a score.
> I confess that I am woefully lacking in the hardihood of aggression; that writing this letter to you is the result of having successfully done battle with a hounding timidity. Having been born in the South and having spent most of my childhood there I believe I can truthfully say that I understand the real Negro music. In some of my work I make use of the idiom undiluted. Again, at other times it merely flavors my themes. And at still other times thoughts come in the garb of the other side of my mixed racial background. I

68. Judith Tick, "Passed Away Is the Piano Girl: Changes in American Musical Life, 1870–1900," in Bowers, Jane and Judith Tick, eds., *Women Making Music: The Western Art Tradition, 1150–1950* (Urbana: University of Illinois Press, 1986), 336–37.

have tried for practical purposes to cultivate and preserve a facility of expression in both idioms, altho I have an unwavering and compelling faith that a national music very beautiful and very American can come from the melting pot just as the nation itself has done.

Will you examine one of my scores?

Yours very sincerely,
(signed) (Mrs.) Florence B. Price

The letter is a masterpiece of economy, decorum, and, in its way, authority. Price tackles the issues of gender and race up-front by mentioning, then dismissing, them. She invites Koussevitzky to set aside prejudice and judge her work on its merits. In making this approach, she reveals her understanding of what she is up against. And she ends her letter with a deeply personal statement, touching on her own character and personal history, the place of "Negro music" in her work, and her firm belief ("unwavering and compelling faith") that she has been a participant in Koussevitzky's own quest to support American composers in their search for a national identity in music. Price's letters to Koussevitzky spanned nine years (1935–44). In October 1944 Koussevitzky did look at one of her scores, but no performances resulted from Price's efforts.[69]

In the 1950s Price's music was being heard throughout the United States and Canada, and she was gaining recognition abroad. Some of these performances came about through her association with the National Association of Negro Musicians. But her career had received a boost in 1940 when she was accepted for membership in the New York-based National Association for American Composers and Conductors, an organization founded in 1933 "to arrange and encourage performances and works by American composers and to help develop understanding and friendly cooperation between composers and conductors."[70] Only a few months later she received a letter from Paul Berthoud of the NAACC with a request for her to send some of her chamber music for a Sunday evening concert series of contemporary American music during the 1940–41 season.[71] Programs have not been located to confirm whether or not any of her music was performed.

In 1951 Price received a telegram from Sir John Barbirolli, conductor of the Hallé Orchestra in Manchester, England, who knew of her work from his time in the United States (1936–42) as conductor of the New York Philharmonic Orchestra. For his orchestra, Barbirolli asked, would Price write a concert overture or suite for strings based on black American spirituals? She would indeed, and she would go to England for the performance. Here was the personal and professional affirmation that had so far eluded her. She began work on the overture immediately. The *Chicago Defender* noted that Price was to have "a number of works" presented in Paris during the "spring season of 1951," as well.[72]

In addition to working on the concert overture, Price completed a *String Quartet on Negro Themes* that was premiered at Carey Temple church in February 1951. This piece may have been the work she later titled *Five Folksongs in Counterpoint*, originally the *Negro Folksongs in Counterpoint*. The *Five Folksongs in Counterpoint* included movements titled "Calvary," "Clementine," "Drink to Me Only With Thine Eyes,"

---

69. Price wrote seven letters to Koussevitzky (8 August 1935, 18 September 1941, 5 July 1943, 6 November 1943, 22 May 1944, 7 June 1944, and 23 October 1944) and she received two letters from Koussevitzky's secretary with responses (17 November 1943 and 31 October 1944). Koussevitzky Collection, Library of Congress, Music Division.

70. Helen D. Gillespie to Florence Price, 26 February 1940. Proc./TS. 1p. Price Materials.

71. Paul Berthoud to Florence Price, 24 September 1940. TS. 1p. Price Materials.

72. Price's friend, Neumon Leighton, explained to Mildred Denby Green that he was present when Price received the cable from England. Green, 34. The Paris trip is mentioned in "Florence Price's Work Spotlighted," *Chicago Defender*, 10 February 1951, 21, and in "Noted Composers' Works to Spark Circle Concert," *Chicago Defender*, 20 January 1951, 24.

Rae Linda Brown

"Shortnin' Bread," and "Swing Low, Sweet Chariot." *Five Folksongs* is not a work for amateur players. Technically challenging, the texture throughout is contrapuntal and conveys to the listener the serious treatment of these songs. The familiar melodies are shared between the instruments equally; thematic phrases are often separated by freely interpolated material. As with much music emanating from the oral tradition, a convincing interpretation of these folksongs requires a flexible approach to rhythm and an understanding of the subtle but fluid phrasing (now detached, now slurred, though not always marked in the score).

Price finished the concert overture, now lost, and she readied herself for Europe. Barbirolli did perform her work in the spring of 1951, but Price was not there to hear it. It appears she was in the hospital for an extended stay. Once her health improved, however, she completed several compositions during the next eighteen months. In addition to finishing the second Violin Concerto, she wrote a chamber work, *Sea Gulls*, for women's chorus or quartet with flute, clarinet, violin, viola, cello, and piano. It was premiered 14 May 1951 at Chicago's Lake View Musical Society's installation of officers. Price's *Suite of Negro Dances*, for orchestra, was performed by the Chicago Symphony Orchestra, led by associate conductor George Schick, on 18 February 1953 on WGN-TV (Channel 9) as part of a live televised "pops" concert. Even the United States Marine Band found something of interest in Price's oeuvre; during the late 1940s and early 1950s it regularly performed the *Three Negro Dances* (a different work than the *Suite*), first made popular by the Michigan WPA Concert Band.[73]

In early 1953 Price planned another trip to Europe. She was to receive an award in Paris in the spring, and she planned to combine it with her long-anticipated vacation to France and England. For this special trip she would take with her Perry Quinney Johnston, her close friend from Little Rock. They would sail from New York for Le Havre, France, on 26 May 1953.[74] Plans were made for her to meet with publishers while in Europe. However, the trip had to be cancelled when Price was hospitalized again. On 3 June 1953, after ten days in the hospital, Florence Price died. Her funeral took place two days later at Grace Presbyterian Church. She is buried in Chicago's Lincoln Cemetery.[75]

The esteem in which members of the black community held Price had been evident as early as 1940, when a third Chicago branch of the National Association of Negro Musicians, the Florence B. Price Music Study Guild, was formed and named after her. Believing that the two older branches of NANM had become too complacent, the Price Music Study Guild had as its mission to raise the performance standards of NANM and to attract larger audiences to its concerts. To reflect the Guild's strong commitment to education, Price herself donated the first gift toward a scholarship fund. Many Chicagoans thought the Price Study Guild had been appropriately named for a musician who stood as a symbol of professional achievement and personal tenacity. The organization was a vibrant one, promoting the musical activities of black classical artists throughout the Midwest. Florence Price walked on ground that no other black woman had trod. The continued performances, new recordings, and publications of her music, and the building of the Florence B. Price Elementary School (dedicated in 1964) in Chicago, are living testimonies to the accomplishments and legacy of this remarkable woman.

---

73. See programs in the Price Materials, University of Arkansas. See also "Noted Composer," *The* [Cleveland] *Plain Dealer*, 11 August 1939, incl. photo.

74. Letter from Price to Perry [Quinney Johnston] dated May, no year. Price Materials. Barbara Garvey Jackson, Professor of Music Emeritus, University of Arkansas, established the date as 1953. The date was confirmed by Marion Quinney Ross, Johnston's daughter.

75. Price died from a cerebral hemorrhage due to hypertensive cardiovascular disease. Medical Certificate of Death, State of Illinois. Filed 3 June 1953. "Florence Price, Noted Composer, Buried Here," *Chicago Defender*, 11 June 1953.

Genesis and Performance Reception

In January 1931, the same month in which Florence Price was granted a divorce from her husband, she began work on the Symphony in E Minor, her first full-scale orchestral composition. The symphony was to occupy much of her time for the next two years. She even welcomed a painful accident that gave her time to compose. In a letter to a friend she wrote: "I found it possible to snatch a few precious days in the month of January in which to write undisturbed. But, oh dear me, when shall I ever be so fortunate again as to break a foot."[76]

In February 1932 Price entered the Rodman Wanamaker Competition. Sponsored by the Robert Curtis Ogden Association and the National Association of Negro Musicians in memory of Rodman Wanamaker (1863–1920), son of department store owner John Wanamaker, the Wanamaker Competition was established in 1927 to offer prizes to African-American composers. Like the Rockefeller and Rosenwald Fellowships, composition prizes offered through *Opportunity* magazine, and the Harmon Foundation Awards, the Wanamaker contest was prestigious and provided long overdue recognition to African-American composers in several categories: songs, piano compositions, and symphonic works. Price submitted four compositions, and each of them won recognition. The Symphony in E Minor took the $500 first prize for an orchestral work, while her tone poem *Ethiopia's Shadow in America* won Honorable Mention in the same category. Price's Piano Sonata in E Minor won the $250 award, while her Fantasie no. 4 for piano won Honorable Mention. The remaining prize money went to Margaret Bonds, Price's friend and former student, who received $250 as first prize in the final category for her song "The Sea Ghost."

Black Chicagoans were thrilled that two of their own had won the Wanamaker awards. Only days after the announcement, the Chicago Music Association started planning a celebration in honor of Price and Bonds at one of their regular Tuesday meetings. Estella Bonds chaired the special program that included community singing led by George Guliatt, a selection by an a cappella woman's quartet known as the Harmonious Four, directed by William Henry Smith, a selection by baritone John Green, and a talk on current topics by Price. In the weeks following the prize announcement Price and Bonds were "showered with letters and expressions of congratulations." It was noted in the press that Price was a bit shy, even "retiring," and winning the Wanamaker prizes was a major achievement that, it was hoped, would now bring her music to the fore.[77]

The prizes brought Price national attention. One who took notice was Frederick Stock, conductor of the Chicago Symphony Orchestra, who, in 1932 was appointed music advisor to the 1933 Chicago World's Fair that was titled "Century of Progress Exhibition." Stock would premiere Price's Symphony in E Minor in the orchestra's initial series of concerts at the Exposition in June 1933.

That Stock took an interest in Price was characteristic of the conductor who had been programming American music and supporting American composers since he became director of the Chicago Symphony in 1905. Stock's enthusiasm for America and American music was unusual for his time. As early as 1914 Stock (born in Prussia in 1872; died in Chicago in 1942) began conducting orchestra rehearsals in English with his primarily German musicians, and by the 1917–18 season he announced that each program would include at least one work by an American composer.[78] Although Stock

---

76. Quoted in notecards #14–16 of Florence Price Robinson, Price Materials, University of Arkansas.

77. See "Music News," *Chicago* Defender, March and April 1933, 15.

78. Dena Epstein, "Frederick Stock and American Music," *American Music* 10/1 (Spring 1992), 29. Stock switched from speaking to the orchestra in German to English in deference to the severe anti-German

Rae Linda Brown

was criticized for his decision to program "too many novelties . . . especially works of American and Chicago writers," he was not deterred from his commitment. In designing the music series for the Fair, he announced that he was interested in "Chicago talent first and American talent second, and [that] . . . European representation will be drastically limited."[79]

The months before the performance of her symphony were hectic for Price. Although she had yet to complete a final copy of the symphony's score and parts, she fulfilled her professional obligations during the remainder of 1932. In October she gave talks on "current events" for two meetings of the Chicago Music Association. In November she gave a talk on black composers and she accompanied soprano Gladys Nelson, also a member of the Chicago Music Association, in a program for the Twentieth Century Club, a white organization. In December the Chicago Music Association visited the rare instrument collection at the Harding Museum, where Price talked about historic organs and performance practice.[80] There, she and Estella Bonds demonstrated the eighteenth- and nineteenth-century pianos while the group sang.[81]

December 1932 was to mark another milestone for Price. Her *Fantasie Negre in E Minor for Piano* (apparently not the same work that won the Wanamaker Honorable Mention) had attracted the attention of Mme. Lumilla Speranzeya, a Russian ballet teacher at the Chicago Art Theater, who choreographed a ballet to Price's work. The dancers were a group working with black choreographer Katherine Dunham, who was interested in forming a permanent dance troupe. The ballet was premiered to much acclaim at the elegant Stevens Hotel Beaux Arts Ball, accompanied by pianist Margaret Bonds who had worked for months with the dancers.[82]

That Bonds was chosen to accompany the dance troupe in the *Fantasie Negre* ballet is not surprising. During the 1930s Bonds became well known for her interpretations of Price's music, which she performed on numerous occasions. Bonds played Price's piano compositions at the local NANM meetings of the Chicago Music Association and she also performed them at national meetings of the organization. As their professional relationship grew, Price and Bonds were asked to perform on the same program. One such occasion was the annual Julius Rosenwald Memorial concert on 12 February 1933. Rosenwald (1862–1932), a wealthy benefactor who established a fellowship for African-American performers (as well as fellowships for law, the social sciences, medicine, journalism, and education), was held in high esteem by the black musical community. For this concert, Price performed the third movement of her organ sonata and Bonds performed solo piano works. The following month, March 1933, Bonds and Price played Price's two-piano arrangement of the spiritual "Sinner Please Don't Let This Harvest Pass" at the Berean Baptist Church. The occasion was a musicale in honor of Marian Anderson, who was in town to perform on NBC radio.[83]

During the early months of 1933 Price worked as a free-lance arranger for baritone Louis White at WGN radio. She also composed small-scale piano pieces, performed on piano and organ, lectured through the city, conducted performances of her Treble

---

sentiment in the United States during World War I. Performing American repertoire helped to balance the orchestra's traditional German fare.

79. Quoted in Epstein, "Frederick Stock and American Music," 29.

80. A significant portion of the Harding Museum's collection was transferred, in 1982, to the Chicago Art Institute.

81. George, "Music News," *Chicago Defender*, 17 December 1932, 15.

82. Ibid.

83. George, "Music News," *Chicago Defender* (11 February 1933; 18 February 1933; 25 March 1933), 15. In 1933 Bonds was a recipient of a Rosenwald Fellowship, which enabled her to pursue a Master's Degree in piano performance at Northwestern University (M.M. 1934). The spiritual "Sinner, Please Don't Let This Harvest Pass" was used by Price in a concert overture, in an arrangement for two pianos, and in the solo piano work *Fantasie Negre* in E Minor.

Clef choir (which sang popular songs, classical choral pieces including those written by her, and arrangements of spirituals and gospel music), and continued work on her symphony. By the end of March, Price withdrew from most of her activities in order to copy the parts of her symphony. Rushing to meet her deadline, she enlisted the help of friends, including Margaret Bonds. Bonds explained: "During the cold winter nights in Chicago, we used to sit around a large table in our kitchen—manuscript paper strewn around, Florence and I extracting parts for some contest deadline. We were a God-loving people, and, when we were pushed for time, every brown-skinned musician in Chicago who could write a note, would 'jump-to' and help Florence meet her deadline."[84]

The time was busy for Margaret Bonds, too. In addition to helping Price copy out orchestra parts, she was preparing the solo part of John Alden Carpenter's Concertino for Piano and Orchestra for a performance with the Chicago Symphony on the same evening that Price's symphony would be played.

Broadcast over NBC radio, on a program featuring "The Negro in Music," the performance of Price's Symphony in E Minor took place on Thursday, 15 June 1933, at Chicago's Auditorium Theater. It was hoped that this historic concert would be held in a new facility on the fair grounds, but the Depression had made this economically unfeasible. The plans underway for a new concert hall had to be laid aside. The Friends of Music, the group that sponsored the Century of Progress Exposition series, chose the Auditorium—the city's largest venue—as the alternate site.

At the conclusion of her symphony, Price, elegantly dressed in a long white gown, was recalled to the stage again and again and acknowledged the enthusiastic applause. Her symphony won critical acclaim, and it marked the first large-scale work by a black woman composer to be played by a major American orchestra. Bonds, too, made history that evening, becoming the first black instrumentalist to appear with the Chicago Symphony.[85]

With the June 1933 Chicago Symphony Orchestra concert, the "Negro in Music" was celebrated both as performer and composer. This concert was recognized as a momentous occasion by Chicago music lovers both black and white. John Alden Carpenter and his wife had brought to the concert special guests; these included George Gerswhin, who had played a concert at the Auditorium Theater just the night before, and diplomat Adlai Stevenson, his wife, and his sister, who were in town from Washington, D.C., to visit the fair.[86] One social critic for the *Chicago Daily Tribune*, detailing the enthusiastic response to the evening, found it appropriate to headline an article: "Black Satin Clothes Seen at Symphony: Many Box Parties at Fair Concert." The article reads, in part: "A large and appreciative audience in the old Auditorium last night cheered Chicago's Symphony orchestra. The hundreds of music lovers enjoyed the symphony in E Minor and John Alden Carpenter's *Concertino* . . . . Not since the eighties [1880s] has there been such a response to [a] summer night musical program."[87]

The concert included the *Overture "In Old Virginia" by* John Powell, Samuel Coleridge-Taylor's *Bamboula*, and John Alden Carpenter's jazzy Concertino for Piano

84. Bonds, "A Reminiscence," 192.

85. The first black soloist with the Chicago Symphony was singer George R. Garner, tenor, who appeared with the orchestra under Frederick Stock in 1924 or 1925. Ellistine Perkins Holly, "Black Concert Music in Chicago, 1890 to the 1930s," *Black Music Research Newsletter* 9/2 (Fall 1987), 6.

86. Adlai Stevenson (1900–65) served one term as governor of Illinois. He ran, unsuccessfully, for president (Democratic Party) in 1952 and 1956. From 1961 until 1965 he served as the U.S. Ambassador to the United Nations.

87. "Black Satin Clothes Seen at Symphony," *Chicago Daily Tribune*, 16 June 1933, 1. This article details Gershwin's visit to Chicago and his attendance at the concert along with the Carpenters, Adlai Stevenson, and other notable guests.

and Orchestra with Margaret Bonds as soloist. The guest artist for the evening was renowned tenor Roland Hayes, who sang the aria "Onaway! Awake, Beloved!" from Coleridge-Taylor's 1898 cantata *Hiawatha's Wedding-Feast* and two spirituals, "Swing Low, Sweet Chariot," arranged and orchestrated by Harry T. Burleigh, and "Bye and Bye," arranged and orchestrated by Hayes. Hayes also performed the aria "Le Repos de la Sainte Famille" from Berlioz's *L'Enfance du Christ*.

The "Century of Progress" concert received reviews in both the black and white press. Nahum Daniel Brascher, writing for the *Chicago Defender*, discussed the progress of "race musicians" to date and the significance of the Chicago Symphony Orchestra performance. He concluded: "The occasion was the very last word in music achievement. For us the last word is the first opportunity. . . . It was successful absolutely on merit, and it is the beginning of a new era for us in the world of music."[88] Robert Abbot, editor of the *Chicago Defender*, amplified Brascher's words when he wrote:

> No one could have sat through that program . . . and not have felt, with a sense of deep satisfaction, that the Race is making progress in music. First there was a feeling of awe as the Chicago Symphony Orchestra, an aggregation of master musicians of the white race, and directed by Dr. Frederick Stock, internationally known conductor, swung in to the beautiful, harmonious strains of a composition by a Race woman. And when, after the number was completed, the large auditorium, filled to the brim with music lovers of all races, rang out in applause for the composer and the orchestral rendition, it seemed that the evening could hold no greater thrills.[89]

It is noteworthy that the editor of the *Chicago Defender* fails to mention Price by name, preferring to accentuate the symbolic cultural significance of the event. Of course, because of the frequent mention of Price's work, personal appearances at music events all over town, and the documented excitement in the community with regard to this performance, the *Defender's* black readers knew who Abbot was referring to; the editor was invoking a kind of common familiarity that bonds the black community. On the other hand, given the uncommonness of this concert, Price's anonymity is striking. That this concert marked the first time that a major orchestra had performed a work by a black woman composer was not mentioned.

It was the white press who, in many ways, validated Price's musical accomplishments as a composer. In contrast to the black press, white critics were little interested in social consciousness or historical significance. For these critics, Price's symphony was the highlight of the concert program, even as Roland Hayes's and Margaret Bonds's performances were enthusiastically received. Glenn Dillard Gunn of the *Chicago Herald & Examiner* commented that "Mrs. Price's symphony proved to be highly interesting to her audience. Its orchestration is handled in orthodox fashion and it 'sounds.' " The music critic for the *Winnetka Talk* praised the symphony and mentioned that "it is believed that an outstanding composer has been discovered."[90]

The critics of the *Music News* and the *Chicago Evening American* were particularly interested in the underlying African-American musical characteristics inherent in the score. The critic from the *Music News* wrote: "Mrs. Price['s] work displayed a distinct flair for composition, and like the good workman and musician that she is, she made use of thematic material and racial characteristics. I found the choral [chorale-like] treatment of the second movement very appealing, and what seemed like a Juba Dance (the scherzo movement) highly exhilarating." The longest review came from Eugene Stinson of the *Chicago Daily News*. He wrote, in part:

> A symphony by Florence Price had its first performance on this occasion. It is a faultless work cast in something less than modernist mode and even reminiscent at times of other

88. Brascher, "Roland Hayes," *Chicago Defender*, 24 June 1933, 11.
89. [Robert Abbot], *Chicago Defender*, 24 June 1933, 11.
90. Music review, *Winnetka Talk* (Winnetka, Ill.), 16 June 1933.

composers who have dealt with America in tone. But for all its dependence upon the idiom of others, it is a work that speaks its own message with restraint and yet with passion. Miss Price's symphony is worthy of a place in the repertory.[91]

The inspiration for Price's Symphony in E Minor was undoubtedly Antonín Dvořák's 1893 Symphony no. 9, "From the New World," also in E Minor. This symphony, like no other, impelled American composers to look seriously at African-American folk materials for their source of creativity. Dvořák was able to capture the pathos of many black spirituals so vividly that many people believe that the soul-stirring, faux-spiritual melody of the Largo second movement is authentic. This movement became famous when William Arms Fisher, one of Dvořák's students at the National Conservatory of Music in New York, fitted the melody with the text known as "Goin' Home."[92]

A second inspiration for Price's symphony, albeit an indirect one, came from the music of the African-British composer Samuel Coleridge-Taylor, who visited the United States three times between 1904 and 1910. Coleridge-Taylor had a keen interest in African-American folk music, an interest that resulted from contacts he made with the African-American poet Paul Laurence Dunbar in 1897 and from hearing the Fisk Jubilee Singers in concert in 1899. Coleridge-Taylor's compositions include the 1905 *Twenty-Four Negro Melodies, Transcribed for the Piano* and the 1906 *Symphonic Variations on an African Air*, based on the spiritual "I'm Troubled in Mind."[93]

Coleridge-Taylor is best known for his trilogy of cantatas based on texts by Henry Wadsworth Longfellow: *Hiawatha's Wedding Feast* from 1898 ("Onaway! Awake, Beloved!" the tenor aria, is its best-known movement), *The Death of Minnehaha* from 1899, and *Hiawatha's Departure* from 1900. His popular *Bamboula*, which concluded the Chicago Symphony concert, was originally written for piano and is based on spirited African dance rhythms. His "Danse negre," the final movement of the 1898 *African Suite* (originally for piano quintet but later orchestrated by the composer), was inspired by a poem written by Dunbar and may well have been a direct influence for Price's *Fantasie Negre* and the juba dance movements of her symphonies.

Analysis

Together with William Grant Still's *Afro-American Symphony* (1930) and William Dawson's *Negro Folk Symphony* (1934), Price's Symphony in E Minor (1931–32) is a work that represents the musical culmination of a "cultural awakening" referred to as the Harlem Renaissance or New Negro Movement. The Negro Renaissance of the 1920s spawned a surge of literary, artistic, and musical creativity by America's black artists. Its affirmation of black cultural heritage had a decisive impact on Price. Her primary goal for the first symphony was to feature Negro folk materials: spiritual-like themes, characteristic dance music, cross-rhythms, call-and-response organizational procedures,

---

91. Glenn Dillard Gunn, *Chicago Herald & Examiner*, 16 June 1933; Herman Devries, *Chicago Evening American*, 16 June 1933; *Winnetka Talk*, 16 June 1933; Eugene Stinson, *Chicago Daily News*, 16 June 1933; E.H.B., *Music New*, 16 June 1933.

92. For a full discussion of Dvořák and the New World Symphony see Joseph Horowitz, "Antonín Dvořák and Charles Ives in Search of America," in *Classical Music in America: A History of Its Rise and Fall* (New York: Norton, 2004), 211–41. See also Michael Beckerman, "Dvořák, Krehbiel, and the 'New World'" (chapter 8) and "Burleigh and Dvořák: From Plantation to the Symphony" (chapter 9) in *New Worlds of Dvořák* (New York: Norton, 2003).

93. The relationship between Coleridge-Taylor and Dunbar has been well documented. See, for example, Percy M. Young, "Samuel Coleridge-Taylor, 1875–1912," *The Musical Times* 116/1590 (August 1975): 703–705. See also "Coleridge-Taylor, Samuel" in the *International Dictionary of Black Composers*, vol. 1, Samuel A. Floyd, Jr., ed. (Chicago: Fitzroy Dearborn Publishers, 1999), 275–85. This essay includes a discussion of *Twenty-Four Negro Melodies* and other works.

Rae Linda Brown

dominance of a percussive, polyrhythmic approach to music, off-beat phrasing of melodic accents, and the inclusion of environmental factors such as hand-clapping and foot-tapping. These African-American nationalist elements are integral to the composition's style. The simple musical structures of the four movements are inherently bound to the folk tradition in which they are rooted.

Dvořák's "New World" Symphony and the spiritual inspiration of Coleridge-Taylor were creative influences on Price's work. Although her score is relatively unknown, her symphony contributes significantly to the American nationalist movement and to the musical legacy of the Harlem Renaissance. Price had become familiar with the use of vernacular elements in serious composition through her studies with Chadwick at the New England Conservatory, but an examination of Price's symphony reveals that she had thoroughly studied Dvořák's score as well. To judge from its overall content, formal organization, orchestration, and spirit, she seems to have taken quite personally the Bohemian composer's directive to create a national composition.

Both Dvořák's and Price's symphonies are in the key of E minor, and both works have subtitles that suggest the inspiration for their primary source material. Originally subtitled the "Negro Symphony," Price's work assimilates characteristic African-American folk idioms into classical structures. Price abandoned the subtitle, possibly because it might have suggested a programmatic work and limited the perception of the symphony's scope.

Price's score specifies a standard romantic-era orchestra (strings, woodwinds, brass, and percussion including harp, timpani, bass drum, and cymbals), but she has augmented the percussion section to include several "special effects" instruments including cathedral chimes, small and large African drums, orchestral bells, and wind whistle.[94]

The first movement of the symphony is structured in sonata form.[95] A six-measure introduction in E minor played by bassoons accompanied by strings becomes the countermelody for the principal theme of the exposition. This theme, announced by solo oboe and clarinet (mm. 7–10), and its countermelody are built on a pentatonic scale, the most frequently used scale in African-American folksongs. The simple harmonization of the theme—i, iv, v, i—grows out of the implied harmony of the theme itself.

A secondary theme (mm. 71–78), in G major, is played first by a French horn accompanied by sustained strings. The treatment of the theme resembles the melodic contour and orchestration of its counterpart in Dvořák's symphony. Written in the same key, Dvořák's melody is played by solo flute, accompanied by strings. This theme marks Price's symphony as derivative and reminiscent of the past. Although relatively short, the melody is indelible. The development section is straightforward. Harmonic and motivic alteration of the themes is explored, and, in contrast to what occurs in the exposition, the texture is primarily contrapuntal. Inversions of the primary and secondary theme take place. A modified recapitulation, in which shortened versions of the themes recur, follows the development.

The second movement of Price's symphony is a hymn in E major. One is struck by the similarity to Dvořák's colorful orchestration. Dvořák's famous Largo melody is framed by an introduction played by clarinets, bassoons, and brass. Price's twenty-eight-measure hymn is played first by a brass choir (four horns, two trumpets, three trombones, and tuba). Price's interest in church music and the idiosyncrasies of organ

---

94. It is not known what Price means by "wind whistle." Whistles, however, are not uncommon in African traditional music. The instruments can be made of a variety of materials including cane and wood. Many of them sound much like flutes.

95. Sonata form is a musical form, characteristic of the first movement of a symphony, having three sections: exposition (with two related key areas and at least one theme for each), development (a tonally unstable section where the themes are altered and may include some new material), and recapitulation (a return to the exposition in the original key).

sound probably also stand behind this instrumentation. Organists will draw a brass chorus on the organ as an alternative to foundation stops in hymn playing. The use of 16-foot reeds produce a colorful but not necessarily overbearing sound.

Like Dvořák's second movement, Price's hymn melody is built on a pentatonic scale (E, F-sharp, G-sharp, B, C-sharp) and sets it in ABA form. The harmonic complexity of the hymn is a departure from African-American folk music. One can observe that this arrangement, while melodically inspired by the spiritual, is solidly rooted in classical Western European instrumental writing. The flutes and clarinets provide short interjections between phrases (providing call-and-response with the hymn melody), while African drums and timpani provide a continual underlying pulse that parallels the verse-and-refrain form common in many African-American spirituals and other sacred music. Of further interest in comparing the two movements is the way solo instruments are featured in both Dvořák's and Price's scores. For the famous Largo melody, Dvořák uses an English horn solo over a chordal string accompaniment. Price's movement includes clarinet and English horn solos sounding fragments of the hymn melody over sustained strings.

Always committed to African-American musical principles, Price turns directly to her roots for the third movement. Titled "Juba Dance," this movement is based on the syncopated rhythms of the antebellum folk dance, "pattin' juba." The dance involves a pattern of foot-tapping, hand-clapping, and thigh-slapping in intricate rhythmic patterns. Typically, slave fiddlers and banjo players would accompany the dancers' percussive body movements. There were several variations to the dance. According to the narrative of Lewis Paine in *Six Years in a Georgia Prison*, written in 1851, "this is done by placing one foot a little in advance of the other, raising the ball of the foot from the ground, and striking it in regular time, while, in connection, the hands are struck slightly together, and then upon the thighs. In this way they make the most curious noise, yet in such perfect order, it furnishes music to dance by."[96]

Solomon Northup, in his autobiography *Twelve Years a Slave*, published in 1853, describes another variation of the dance. He wrote: "[It was] accompanied with one of those unmeaning songs, composed rather for its adaptation to certain tune measure, than for the purpose of expressing any distinct idea. The patting is performed by striking the hands on the knees, then striking the hands together, then striking the right shoulder with one hand, the left with the other—all the while keeping time with the feet and singing."[97]

Price was not the first African-American composer to use the juba as the basis of an instrumental work. The most popular instrumental version of the juba in the early twentieth century was R. Nathaniel Dett's *In the Bottoms* piano suite, published by Clayton F. Summy in 1913, which Price surely would have known. Price included the juba dance in several of her works. In addition to the third movement of the Symphony in E Minor, it is the basis of the third movement of her Symphony in C Minor. The syncopated rhythms are also used in the final section of the Piano Concerto in One Movement (1934) and the third dance from the *Three Negro Dances* for band (1939). Several works for piano, including "Ticklin' Toes" from the third dance from *Three Little Negro Dances* (1933) and "Silk Hat and Walking Cane" from *Dances in the Canebrakes* (1953), are also based on this folk dance.

---

96. Paine was neither a slaveholder nor an abolitionist. He was imprisoned for aiding a slave in escape. Lewis Paine, "Six Years in a Georgia Prison," in Eileen Southern, ed., *Readings in Black American Music*, 2nd ed. (New York: Norton, 1983), 89.

97. Solomon Northup, "Twelve Years a Slave," in Eileen Southern, ed., *Readings in Black American Music*, 2nd ed. (New York: Norton, 1983), 100. Northup was born a free man and then was kidnapped into slavery. Born in Saratoga Springs, New York, he was a dance fiddler of some repute. Northup was lured to the south where he was sold into slavery by traveling entrepreneurs who had engaged his professional services as a musician.

Rae Linda Brown

Price sets the juba dance movement in rondo form, and thus features a recurrent theme alternating with new material. In the A section, the violins present a sprightly, syncopated eight-measure rhythmic motive, simulating what might have been played by an antebellum fiddler. Against it, a pizzicato "oom-pah" bass is provided by a tonic-dominant ostinato in the remaining strings and percussion. The rhythms that form the basis of the dance are African-derived, entering the juba dance by way of black banjo and fiddle music with its percussive accompaniment of hand-clapping and foot-tapping.

The last movement of the symphony, marked Finale, is the most straightforward. A duple meter Presto in E minor, its melodic-harmonic content is based on a four-measure triplet figure that ascends and descends around a natural minor scale built on the pitch E. Flutes, oboes, and violins render the unison line while the orchestra accompanies with sparse chords. The general form of the fourth movement loosely resembles a rondo.

The absence of overt identifiable ethnic characteristics in the Symphony in E Minor, such as quotations of black folk themes or the use of a blues progression, caused Alain Locke, an ardent spokesman of the Harlem Renaissance, to criticize the work in his 1936 essay "The Negro and His Music." Locke discussed Price's symphony as though it had no racial references, asserting:

> In straight classical idiom and form, Mrs. Price's work vindicates the Negro composer's right, at choice, to go up Parnassus by the broad high road of classicism rather than the narrower, more hazardous, but often more rewarding path of racialism. At the pinnacle, the paths converge, and the attainment becomes, in the last analysis, neither racial nor national, but universal music.[98]

Locke's evaluation of black music depended on whether or not it evoked identifiable black musical traits. While this approach may be valuable, it limits the scope of the black music tradition. When one examines Price's symphony, it becomes evident that Price's music is reflective of her cultural heritage.

As an examination of Price's symphony has revealed, by no means did she exclude racial elements. In addition to the African-American materials already discussed, Price adapts fundamental conceptual approaches to African-American music to the symphonic idiom. For example, she transforms the polyrhythmic manner of approaching rhythm and the inclusion of environmental factors into musical entities in the juba dance of the third movement. The steady accompaniment to the melody is a direct manifestation of physical body movements that were the essence of "pattin' juba."

Olly Wilson and other scholars of African-American music have pointed out that the sound ideal in African-American music is a heterogeneous one.[99] A tendency to maintain an independence of voices by means of timbral differentiation, or stratification, is common. Nowhere in Price's symphony is this more clear than in the second movement where tonal colors of the brass choir and woodwind ensemble are juxtaposed with large and small African drums, cathedral chimes, and orchestral bells. Call-and-response interchange, a core trait of African-American music, is also exhibited in this movement between the brass choir and the woodwind ensemble.

African-American cultural characteristics are also borne out implicitly in the themes of the first movement. Its opening is based on a pentatonic scale, one of the

---

98. Alain Locke, *The Negro and His Music* (New York: Arno Press and the *New York Times*, [ca. 1936] 1969), 114.

99. Olly Wilson has written extensively on the characteristics of African-American music. His articles include "The Significance of the Relationship Between Afro-American and West African Music," *The Black Perspective in Music* 2/1 (Spring 1974): 3–22; "Black Music as an Art Form," *Black Music Research Journal* 3 (1983): 1–22; and "Composition from the Perspective of the African-American Tradition," *Black Music Research Journal* 16/1 (Spring 1996): 43–51.

most frequently used scales in African-American music. The preference for duple meter with syncopated rhythms and altered tones (malleable third and seventh scale degrees, the so-called "blue notes") are also specific features of African-American music that characterize the melodies of this movement. These traits in themselves may not be exclusive to black music, as Wilson observes, but in combination they are fundamental to the African-American music tradition. Price's approach to composition derives essentially from African-American musics, and the predominance of these core characteristics is the best evidence for this.

Racial pride was quintessential to the Harlem Renaissance and the black nationalist movement in music during that era. It was this attitude that permeated much of Florence Price's music of the 1930s. Harlem Renaissance ideals, and those of the New Negro Movement, form the background against which she developed as a composer.

SYMPHONY NO. 3 IN C MINOR

Genesis

During the early 1930s, musicians were especially hard hit by the economic effects of the Great Depression. The rise of radio in the 1920s had decreased opportunities for performing musicians. And with the advent of sound film in 1927, work available in movie theaters gradually evaporated. In the years between 1929 and 1934, approximately seventy percent of all musicians in the United States were unemployed.[100] In 1935, the government responded by establishing, chiefly as a relief measure, the Federal Music Project for unemployed musicians under the auspices of the Works Progress Administration (WPA), later renamed the Works Projects Administration.[101]

As things worked out, the difficulties of the private sector, sparking the advent of a publicly funded government agency for music, proved a boon for black artists. Some of Price's most important works were written during the WPA years. In addition, the careers of composers William Grant Still, Clarence Cameron White, Julian Work and his brother John Work III, Harry T. Burleigh, R. Nathaniel Dett, Carl Diton, W. C. Handy, and Eva Jessye were supported to some degree through the performances by WPA ensembles. Ralph Ellison explains that national disasters like the Great Depression also brought certain benefits with them, such as

> the possibility for a broader Afro-American freedom. This is a shocking thing to say, but it is also a very blues, or tragicomic, thing to say, and a fairly accurate description of the manner in which, for Negroes, a gift of freedom arrived wrapped in the guise of disaster. . . . The WPA provided an important surge to Afro-American cultural activity. The result was not a "renaissance," but there was a resuscitation and transformation of that very vital artistic impulse that is abiding among Afro-Americans. . . . Afro-American cultural style is an abiding aspect of our culture, and the economic disaster which brought the WPA gave it an accelerated release and allowed many Negroes to achieve their identities as artists.[102]

Although the Federal Music Project was an attempt to cope with unemployment, it also produced new forms of educational and cultural activity that placed emphasis on

---

100. Richard Crawford, *America's Musical Life: A History* (New York: Norton, 2001), 590.

101. Established in 1935 by President Franklin Delano Roosevelt, the Works Progress Administration was renamed the Works Projects Administration in 1939. Its programs included the Federal Art Project, the Federal Music Project, the Federal Writers' Project, and the Federal Theater Project. Musical performances averaged 4,000 a month. At one time, there were 3.5 million people employed by the WPA. The involvement of the United States in World War II led to drastic cuts and in June 1943 the agency was closed permanently.

102. Ralph Ellison, *Going to the Territory* (New York: Random House, 1986), 204–5.

Rae Linda Brown

fostering American music and seeking to connect home-grown classical composers more closely to American communities. One such enterprise was the Composers Forum-Laboratory, established in the fall of 1935 by Dr. Nikolai Sokoloff, the National Director of the WPA Music Project. Under the leadership of Sokoloff, more than 6,000 American works were presented.[103] The activity of the Composers Forum was nationwide. Radio programs presented new compositions first heard in workshop sessions; lectures, too, were offered to the public.

At a concert on 15 June 1937 the Forum String Quartet, made up of faculty from the University of Illinois, participated in a performance of Price's *The Wind and the Sea* (1934), an octet for piano quintet and vocal ensemble. Price played the piano part with the quartet. Written for the Dett Mixed Ensemble of the R. Nathaniel Dett Club in Chicago, the octet had been given a less than satisfactory premiere two years earlier because of the work's difficulty. Price's Piano Quintet in E Minor (1936), with local pianist Marion Hall, was also performed, and receiving its premiere performance that same evening was Price's *Fantasie Negre no. 4 in B Minor* (1932), again with Hall as pianist. These pieces are among Price's most serious chamber works. It is unfortunate that none of the works programmed on this concert survive.

Outside Chicago, Price became acquainted with musicians in the Michigan WPA and benefited considerably from two of their ensembles. The 52-piece Detroit WPA Concert Band performed her *Three Negro Dances*.[104] Under the direction of Murdoch J. Macdonald the band brought this work to thousands who heard it for free in auditoriums and parks. Price received her widest exposure from the Michigan WPA Symphony Orchestra. Organized in early 1936, it was known as the Detroit Civic Orchestra; in 1939 it became an integral part of the Michigan Works Projects Administration. Valter Poole made his first appearance with the orchestra during the 1937–38 season and became the orchestra's regular conductor in 1938. Before his appointment with the orchestra, Poole was acting district supervisor of music in the Detroit Public Schools and a violist with the Detroit Symphony Orchestra. He remained with the Civic Orchestra until its dissolution around 1942. Poole premiered Price's Symphony no. 3 on 6 November 1940 with the Michigan WPA Symphony Orchestra at the Detroit Institute of Arts. Also featured on the program was Price as soloist in her Piano Concerto in One Movement (1934).

Like the Symphony in E Minor and the Piano Concerto in One Movement, the Symphony no. 3 earned critical acclaim. J. D. Callaghan, writing for the *Detroit Free Press*, was particularly impressed by the symphony's underlying theme of regional Americanism:

---

103. While the Composers' Forum-Laboratory offered performance opportunities for established composers, its most important single contribution was providing composers with opportunities to hear their work and to benefit from the critiques of their colleagues. In New York, for example, more than 150 composers had their works premiered through this avenue; they included Marion Bauer, Amy Beach, Marc Blitzstein, Aaron Copland, Carlos Chavez, Ruth Crawford, David Diamond, Howard Hanson, Walter Piston, William Schuman, and Virgil Thomson. Ashley Pettis, "The WPA and the American Composer," *Musical Quarterly* (January 1940), 101–12. For more information on the WPA music programs see Lorraine M. Faxio, "The Music Program of the Works Progress Administration: A Documentation and Description of Its Activities with Special Reference to Afro-Americans," in *More Than Dancing: Essays on Afro-American Music and Musicians*, edited by Irene V. Jackson and prepared under the auspices of the Center for Ethnic Music, Howard University (Westport, Conn.: Greenwood Press, 1985). Also see "WPA Orchestras Preserve Living Music, Says Director," *Detroit News*, 10 May 1938; and Ralph Holmes, "Sokoloff Praises WPA Music Work in Michigan," *The Detroit Times*, 10 May 1938.

104. This work was originally written for piano and published by Presser in 1939. It was arranged for band by Erik W. G. Leidzen in 1939. See "Noted Composer," *The* [Cleveland] *Plain Dealer*, 11 August 1939, incl. photo. This work was also played by the U.S. Marine Band from 1939 and was programmed over the American Broadcasting Company's network in July 1953 as part of a concert dedicated to the American Band Movement.

Mrs. Price, both in the concerto and in the symphony, spoke in the musical idiom of her own people, and spoke with authority. There was inherent in both works all the emotional warmth of the American Negro, so that the evening became one of profound melodic satisfaction.

In the symphony there was a slow movement of majestic beauty, a third in which the rhythmic preference of the Negro found scope in a series of dance forms, and a finale which swept forward with great vigor. The third movement was named Juba by the composer, as a tribute to the African dances which were its inspiration.[105]

In the spring of 1941, soon after the performance of her Symphony no. 3, Price and her two daughters moved to an apartment in the Abraham Lincoln Center, a settlement house located at 700 Oakwood Boulevard. The Lincoln Center, lodging for low- to moderate-income people, was a community for teachers, writers, artists, and other African Americans interested in culture and the arts. Even before Price moved to the Lincoln Center, it had become a magnet for writers and artists whose work pushed the boundaries of mainstream subject matter and expression. Here they could explore the new in the company of like-minded artists. The Lincoln Center was the site where the South Side Writers' Group met from 1936–38, first under the leadership of Richard Wright, and then with Margaret Walker. This group was an important one. It consisted of about twenty black writers, all at early stages of their careers, who met weekly at the Center to read aloud and discuss their works-in-progress. Most important, they explored the potential of their work for its broader theoretical implications of black art.

At the time Wright formed the South Side Writers' Group, he was employed on the Illinois Writers' Project, arguably one of the most impressive units of the WPA. In 1939, Arna Bontemps, who had been introduced to the Writers' Project by Wright in 1936, was hired to supervise the production of a local history called *The Negro in Illinois*. The list of writers employed by the project includes some of the most gifted in the United States. Besides Wright, Bontemps, and Margaret Walker, they included Katherine Dunham, a talented writer although better known as a dancer and choreographer, novelist Willard Motley, and short story writer and novelist Frank Yerby. Studs Terkel, who later hosted a long-running radio program in the city, and the young novelist Saul Bellow were among the whites who joined the group.

Scholars have argued that the authors of that project were part of a second flowering of black arts and letters known as the Chicago Renaissance that flourished from 1935 to 1950. Richard Bone posits that a generation of black writers, almost all living in Chicago, came to maturity during that time and created works central to black culture yet different in philosophical and political ideology from the generation that came before it, the so-called Harlem Renaissance or New Negro Movement.[106] The Chicago School evolved as an extension of the Harlem Renaissance, though ideologically distinct from it. Thus the continuum of black arts and letters in the first half of the century is of greater significance than is usually understood by those who confine their attention to the Harlem Renaissance.

The central figure of the Chicago Renaissance was Richard Wright, whose second novel, *Native Son* (1940), based on his experience in Chicago's ghettos, had a dramatic impact on black writing during this time. Arna Bontemps's novel *Black Thunder* (1936), Margaret Walker's volume of poetry *For My People* (1942), and Gwendolyn Brooks's collection *A Street in Bronzeville* (1945) and Pultizer Prize-winning *Annie Allen* (1949) can be included in the movement, as can the work of sociologist Horace Cayton who, with St. Clair Drake, wrote *Black Metropolis* (1945). With an introduction by Richard Wright, this book stands as a seminal study of black migration to Chicago.

---

105. J. D. Callaghan, *Detroit Free Press*, 7 November 1940.

106. Robert Bone, "Richard Wright and the Chicago Renaissance," *Callaloo* 9/3 (Summer 1986), 446–68. In Bone's view, this diversity requires that black literature of the period be reexamined and placed in a broader context.

Why did Chicago prove to be so fertile for this group of writers? By 1930 the South Side of Chicago constituted the second largest concentration of black people in America, exceeded only by New York's Harlem. Most of them flooded the city from the South in search of work and opportunity. Moreover, the economic crisis of the Depression created commonalties among blacks and whites, who had previously lived and worked in segregated environments. The Great Migration, the Depression, and the adjustment to urban life provided these writers with vivid life experiences as subject matter for their art. Their political and sociological framework was integrationist, a view supported by the pioneering urban research of Robert Park and his student Horace Cayton. Cayton's home became a gathering place for Chicago's young black intellectuals and for those artists visiting from out of town, including Langston Hughes who spent weeks at a time in Chicago during the 1930s and early 1940s. Price was not involved directly with Bontemps, Wright, or others on the WPA writer's projects, but her Symphony no. 3 in C Minor reveals the influence of their attitudes and writings on her work.

Analysis

Price thought about and worked on her Symphony no. 3 for several years. In this work she turned away from the compositional procedures she had used in the past; she no longer composed melodies and rhythms closely aligned with African-American spirituals and black folk dance. In a letter to Frederick Schwass, an administrator of the Michigan WPA orchestra, she explained the genesis of the symphony this way:

> My dear Mr. Schwass:
>   I have your letter of October 21. The Symphony No. 3 in C Minor was composed in the late summer of 1938, laid aside for a year and then revised. It is intended to be Negroid in character and expression. In it no attempt, however, has been made to project Negro music solely in the purely traditional manner. None of the themes are adaptations or derivations of folk songs.
>   The intention behind the writing of this work was a not too deliberate attempt to picture a cross section of present-day Negro life and thought with its heritage of that which is past, paralleled or influenced by concepts of the present day.[107]

In her large-scale works, Price conceived of the orchestra as a vehicle for romantic sonority. Her first full-length symphonic works, the Symphony in E Minor and the Piano Concerto in One Movement, use a medium-sized orchestra with woodwinds in twos. After the mid-1930s, Price expanded the orchestral forces to include piccolo, three flutes, two oboes, English horn, two clarinets in B-flat, bass clarinet, two bassoons, four horns, three trumpets in B-flat, three trombones, tuba, harp, percussion, and strings. The percussion writing is especially colorful; along with timpani, in the second movement the Symphony no. 3 requires orchestral bells, snare drum, bass drum, cymbals, triangle, and celeste, and in the third movement (another juba) the battery includes wood blocks, castanets, tambourines, xylophone, and sand blocks.

Texturally, the Symphony no. 3 distinguishes itself in significant ways from Price's earlier works. Although her predilection for melodic writing still abounds, the orchestral writing shows a maturing grasp of orchestral technique. Gone are multiple doublings of the thematic material with chordal accompaniments and simple textures. Here, in melody-with-accompaniment textures as in contrapuntal ones, the melody is an integral part of the sonic fabric. As a result, the thematic development is pushed further in this symphony than in its predecessor, leading to more counterpoint. In addition to the larger orchestra, Price further explores her fondness for instrumental choirs with call-and-response technique, particularly in the second movement.

---

107. Florence B. Price to Frederick L. Schwass, 22 October 1940. TS copy. 1p. Price Materials.

The opening movement, in sonata-allegro form, begins with a moderately paced andante introduction in which descending chromatic chords in C minor (played by woodwinds and brass) set an ominous tone. With a change in tempo to a brisk allegro, the primary theme is tossed between the lower and upper strings (mm. 19–30). This pentatonic theme is spiritual-like, but the source of the melody is obscured by ambiguous harmonies. Interrupting the thematic discourse is a two-measure phrase in the flutes set as a whole tone scale. Such harmonic ambiguity is unusual for Price. This new compositional direction conveys a less conservative approach to the incorporation of black folk music and its style into large-scale works.

The primary theme is ultimately absorbed into an extended bridge that is interrupted by a false second theme, played by the strings, in G minor (mm. 45–52). Here the harmonic rhythm is slower and the tranquil melody is colored by the flatted fifth, raised sixth, and raised seventh scale degrees. A lyrical second theme emerges in E-flat major (mm. 78–87). A pentatonic melody is also heard, its beauty and richness contrasting markedly with the primary theme. Price's interest in orchestral color is evident here. First announced by the trombone, the second theme weaves its way through the brass to an echo of the theme in a woodwind choir.

The tonal ambiguity of the primary theme, its subsidiary themes, and the lengthy chromatic bridge that follows provide ample material for a further working out in the short development section. The second theme is not here at all; the recapitulation follows in the expected manner, omitting the "false" second theme. Price then launches into a coda of forty-one measures, in the tradition of Beethoven. Full of development, this multisectional conclusion continues to explore the potential of the materials in reverse order from that in which they were first presented. Beginning with the second theme, the themes are dramatically subjected to augmentation and diminution over four distinct changes in tempo and meter: moderato assai, 2/2; tempo moderato, 3/2; andante, 4/4; and allegro, 4/4.

Like the second movement of the Symphony in E Minor, the second movement of the Symphony no. 3, marked "andante ma non troppo," features antiphonal choirs of instruments. This quasi-rondo movement is rich with beautiful melodies bathed in orchestral color. The influence of impressionism is clear. The melodies are often accompanied by parallel chords, and phrases end without their expected resolutions. The A section, in A-flat major, presents two melodies. First an oboe solo, accompanied by the lower woodwinds (English horn, clarinets, and bassoons), sings the eight-measure theme, which is immediately spun out further by the string choir. Played by a solo bassoon, the spiritual-like second theme emerges as a pentatonic melody based on F. Again choirs of instruments are explored; the theme is repeated by a woodwind choir, then heard in a tutti orchestra before it dissipates through the brass choir and finally to the strings alone.

The B section begins in the unexpected and far-removed key of G major (mm. 61–65). A rather simple theme, suggesting popular music, is rendered first by brass choir and celeste. But an abrupt digression to a dissonant polytonal passage based on a whole-tone scale in the strings dispels any apparent lightheartedness. The movement ends with a plagal cadence suspended over the final eight bars. One might recall that the hymn of the second movement of Price's first symphony evoked the spirituality of the church; the final "Amen" cadence here seems a conscious attempt to do the same.

The rhythms of the antebellum juba dance again form the basis of the rondo-form third movement. But this juba movement differs significantly from its orchestral predecessors. In both the Symphony in E Minor and the Piano Concerto in One Movement the rhythmic foundation was clearly established at the outset: one group of instruments, usually the lower strings, maintained the steady pulse while another group of instruments—the upper strings, for example—provided the syncopated melody that, combined with the pulse, characterizes the movement of the dance. Here no steady pulse can be found. Rather, Price has added an array of percussion instruments—

tambourine, sand block, wood block, castanets, snare and bass drums, cymbals, and xylophone—to accentuate the rhythmic impulses underlying the dance.[108] Polyrhythmic configurations are prevalent in the dance movements of the Symphony in E Minor and Piano Concerto, but nowhere in Price's orchestral music are the complexities of African-American rhythm more clearly demonstrated than in this movement. The implied metric organization of the first violin melody creates cross-rhythms with the percussion, particularly in measures where the syncopation in the snare drum becomes more complex. Characteristic of the African concept of musical time, equality is given to melody and rhythm; a varying degree of rhythmic clash between a melody and its accompaniment is a feature fundamental to the music of African-American dance.

Another feature of the third movement's opening measures is the irregular phrasing that complements the metric organization. The primary theme of the rondo consists essentially of nine measures subdivided into two four-bar phrases with a one-bar interruption.

In both the Symphony in E minor and the Piano Concerto, the juba movement is harmonically simple. In the Symphony no. 3, in E-flat major, the movement's colorful chords immediately pique the listener's interest. The entire progression—$I/I/IV\flat7/vi7/V^6_4/V^7,VII/I^6_4$—sounds very much like a jazz progression. Although Price was not herself a jazz musician, hearing jazz all around her in Chicago does seem to have had an unconscious impact on some of her compositions.

The rondo includes two episodes. The first presents a tune in the flutes whose melodic contour is related to the A theme; the second is marked by changes in tempo, key, and meter. A lyrical brass choir, marked "andantino," with an underlying rhythmic accompaniment in the strings, provides a contrast in mood. An interesting instrumental combination in this episode is solo flute and xylophone accompanied by sustained violins and pizzicato low strings with trumpets.[109] Throughout this episode in Price's symphony, the listener will be reminded both of Gershwin's popular music and the Latin American habanera dance, which had been introduced to American popular music, including jazz, as early as 1910.

Like the finale of the Symphony in E minor, the last movement of the Symphony no. 3 is a sonata-form scherzo in 6/8, but the latter is more concise and better crafted. The primary themes of both movements are built around a triplet figure that outlines the tonic, but the added seventh in the later symphony gives the otherwise ordinary figure much-needed flavor. The differences in the textures of the two movements are striking. The texture in the last movement of the Symphony in E minor consists essentially of a flute melody doubled by oboes and violins, while the remaining woodwinds, brass, and strings provide an accompaniment of block chords. The opening of the last movement of the Symphony in C minor, like the symphony's other movements, features antiphonal choirs (in canon, with strings answered by woodwinds). Modal mixture is a prominent feature of the secondary theme in G major/minor, first heard in the English horn doubled by the first trombone and accompanied by strings.

After a classic-style repeat of the exposition, the development ensues in G major/minor. Neither the primary nor the secondary theme is developed melodically. Rather, they are fragmented and repeated on different tonal centers, occasionally with chromatic alterations. At one point the themes are combined: one is played in C major by bassoons and cellos while the other is played in G minor by flutes and clarinets.

---

108. In the score, the rhythm of the percussion is notated precisely. However, the individual percussionist is to decide which instrument(s) is (are) used where.

109. By 1940 the vibraphone had a strong association with jazz. Red Norvo, who was based in Chicago and toured with Paul Whiteman, had established the xylophone as a viable jazz instrument in the 1920s.

The straightforward recapitulation concludes with a seventy-measure coda, the longest ending in any movement of Price's orchestral music. Essentially a prolongation of the dominant, it features crescendos that begin in the lowest strings and sweep through the full orchestra. And as if to tease listeners further, isolated instruments play fragments of the primary and secondary themes before "taking off" again through chromatic arpeggios, only to be temporarily interrupted by tutti *sforzando* chords. The movement concludes with a change in tempo and meter—to andante, 4/4—that accentuates the modal mixtures that have been a feature of this movement. In these measures, woodwinds, brass, and lower strings oscillate between C major and C minor against a two-octave descending and ascending chromatic scale in the violins. The movement concludes with three emphatic C minor chords.

Price's 18 September 1941 letter to Serge Koussevitzky, conductor of the Boston Symphony Orchestra, provides a concluding thought on the substance of this work. She wrote:

> I have a symphony in which I tried to portray a cross section of Negro life and psychology as it is today, influenced by urban life north of the Mason and Dixon line. It is not "program" music. I merely had in mind the life and music of the Negro of today and for that reason treated my themes in a manner different from what I would have done if I had centered my attention upon the religious themes of antebellum days, or yet the rag-time and jazz which followed; rather a fusion of these, colored by present cultural influences.[110]

Price's letter marks her growth and change as a composer. While still steeped in the African-American tradition, the Symphony no. 3 offers a more modern approach than does the Symphony in E Minor—a contemporary synthesis of black life and culture rather than a retrospective view of it. R. Nathaniel Dett explained it this way when he wrote: "As it is quite possible to describe the traits, habits, and customs of a people without using the vernacular, so it is similarly possible to musically portray racial peculiarities without the use of national tunes or folk-songs."[111] Price no longer had the need to write overtly black themes and underscore them with simple dance rhythms. The Symphony no. 3 reflects a maturity of style and a new attitude toward black musical materials and the relationship of the black artist to American society.

110. Florence B. Price to Dr. Serge Koussevitzky, 18 October 1941. Koussevitzky Collection, Library of Congress.

111. Black folk music *per se* is not national; Dett is referring to the quotation of black folk themes in large-scale works. R. Nathaniel Dett, *In the Bottoms: Characteristic Suite for the Piano* (Chicago: Clayton F. Summy [1915], 1973), 33.

PLATE 1. First page of holograph score of Florence Price's Symphony no. 1 in E Minor, including a reduction ("for reader's convenience only") with labels for "Basic motive" and "Prin[cipal] Theme." (Florence Price Collection, David W. Mullins Library, University of Arkansas, Fayetteville, Arkansas; used by permission.)

PLATE 2. Mm. 6–13 of the third movement ("Juba") of Florence Price's Symphony no. 3 in C Minor. (James Weldon Johnson Collection, Beinecke Rare Book Library, Yale University, New Haven, Connecticut; used by permission.)

PLATE 3. Florence Price, 1906, while a student at the New England Conservatory in Boston. (Photographer unknown; gifted to Rae Linda Brown by Josephine Harreld Love.)

SYMPHONY NO. 1 IN E MINOR

INSTRUMENTS

Piccolo 1, 2
Flute 1, 2
Oboe, 1, 2
Clarinet 1, 2 in A
Bassoon 1, 2

Horn 1, 2, 3, 4 in F
Trumpet 1, 2 in A
Trombone 1, 2, 3
Tuba

Timpani
Percussion (Snare Drum, Cymbal, Bass Drum, Triangle, Large and Small African Drums, Crash Cymbals, Wind Whistle, Celesta, Cathedral Chimes, Orchestral Bells)

Violin 1, 2
Viola
Violoncello
Contrabass

I

Allegro [ma] non troppo
rit.
Piccolo 1, 2
Flute 1, 2
Oboe 1, 2
Clarinet 1, 2
in A
Bassoon 1, 2
[1]
mp
mf
pp
Horn 1, 2
in F
Horn 3, 4
in F
Trumpet 1, 2
in A
Trombone 1, 2
Trombone 3
Tuba
Timpani
Cymbal
Bass Drum
Allegro [ma] non troppo
rit.
Violin 1
Violin 2
Viola
Violoncello
Contrabass
pizz.
p
mp
pp
[mp]
[p]
[pp]

Florence Price

17
Fl. 1, 2
Ob. 1, 2
Cl. 1, 2 in A
Bn. 1, 2
Hn. 1, 2 in F
Hn. 3, 4 in F
Tpt. 1, 2 in A
Trb. 1, 2
Trb. 3 Tb.
Timp.
Vn. 1
Vn. 2
Va.
Vc.
Cb.
[a 2]
a 2
[non div.]
[arco]
[pizz.]
[div.]

23
Picc. 1, 2
Fl. 1, 2
[a 2]
[p]
Ob. 1, 2
[a 2]
[p]
Cl. 1, 2 in A
a 2
p
cresc. poco a poco
Bn. 1, 2
Hn. 1, 2 in F
Hn. 3, 4 in F
Tpt. 1, 2 in A
p
cresc. poco a poco
Trb. 1, 2
[p]
Trb. 3 Tb.
[p]
Timp.
p [cresc. poco a] poco
Vn. 1
p
cresc. poco a poco
Vn. 2
p
cresc. poco a poco
Va.
[p] [cresc. poco a poco
[unis.]
Vc.
p
cresc. poco a poco
Cb.
[f] cresc. poco a poco

27
I
Picc. 1, 2
Fl. 1, 2
Ob. 1, 2
Cl. 1, 2 in A
Bn. 1, 2
[ff]
Hn. 1, 2 in F
Hn. 3, 4 in F
Tpt. 1, 2 in A
Trb. 1, 2
Trb. 3 Tb.
Timp.
Vn. 1
Vn. 2
Va.
Vc.
Cb.
ff
[>]

Florence Price

35
meno mosso
Picc. 1, 2
Fl. 1, 2
Ob. 1, 2
Cl. 1, 2
in A
Bn. 1, 2
Hn. 1, 2
in F
Hn. 3, 4
in F
Tpt. 1, 2
in A
a 2
Trb. 1, 2
Trb. 3
Tb.
Timp.
Cym.
B. Dr.
meno mosso
Vn. 1
Vn. 2
div.
Va.
[div.]
[unis.]
Vc.
div.
Cb.

Florence Price

45
Tempo primo
accel. poco a poco
Ob. 1, 2
Cl. 1, 2 in A
Bn. 1, 2
[mf]
[cresc. poco a poco
Vn. 1
Vn. 2
Va.
Vc.
mf
cresc.
poco
a
poco
49
a tempo
mp cresc. molto
ff
[ff]
[mp]
a 2
1
Hn. 1, 2 in F
Hn. 3, 4 in F
Timp.
[f]
[tr]
8va
mp

Florence Price

61
Fl. 1, 2
Ob. 1, 2
Cl. 1, 2 in A
Bn. 1, 2
[1]
p
mp
67
[mf]
mf
Hn. 1, 2 in F
Trb. 3 Tb.
[Tb.]
pp
Vn. 1
Vn. 2
Va.
Vc.
div.
Cb.

Florence Price

85
Fl. 1, 2
Ob. 1, 2
Cl. 1, 2 in A
Vn. 1
Vn. 2
Va.
Vc.
Cb.
[1]
[div.]
[non div.]
div.
91
[unis.]
cresc.
[cresc.]

Florence Price

108
1
Picc. 1, 2
[mf]
Fl. 1, 2
Ob. 1, 2
Cl. 1, 2
in A
Bn. 1, 2
[mf]
Hn. 1, 2
in F
[mf]
Hn. 3, 4
in F
[mf]
Tpt. 1, 2
in A
Trb. 1, 2
[mf]
Trb. 3
Tb.
[mf]
Timp.
Vn. 1
Vn. 2
[unis.]
Va.
[unis.]
Vc.
Cb.

Florence Price

a tempo
117
Picc. 1, 2
Fl. 1, 2
Ob. 1, 2
Cl. 1, 2 in A
Bn. 1, 2
Hn. 1, 2 in F
Hn. 3, 4 in F
Tpt. 1, 2 in A
Trb. 1, 2
Trb. 3 Tb.
Timp.
a tempo
Vn. 1
Vn. 2
Va.
Vc.
Cb.
[1]
[p]
[1]
[p]
[1]
mp
p
[div.]
p
mp
[div.]
p
p
mp
[div.]
[unis.]
pp
mp
mp
[div.]
[p]
mp
mp
[mp]
[mp]

123
Fl. 1, 2
Ob. 1, 2
Cl. 1, 2 in A
Bn. 1, 2
Vn. 1
Vn. 2
Va.
Vc.
Cb.
[1]
[a 2]
[unis.]
[div.]
pp
mp
mf
p
[p]
[pp]
[mp]
[mf]
129
Trb. 1, 2
Trb. 3 Tb.
Trb. 3
a 2
div.

135
Fl. 1, 2
Ob. 1, 2
Cl. 1, 2 in A
Bn. 1, 2
Hn. 1, 2 in F
Hn. 3, 4 in F
Tpt. 1, 2 in A
Trb. 1, 2
Trb. 3 Tb.
Vn. 1
Vn. 2
Va.
Vc.
Cb.
mp
mf dim.
[1]
tr
[mf] dim.
mf [dim.]
[a 2]
mf
mf [dim.]
[mf] [dim.]
dim.
[dim.]
[unis.]
[div.]
p
[mf]
[mp]

Florence Price

152
rit.
a tempo
Fl. 1, 2
Ob. 1, 2
Cl. 1, 2 in A
[a 2]
Bn. 1, 2
[a 2]
Hn. 1, 2 in F
Hn. 3, 4 in F
Tpt. 1, 2 in A
Trb. 1, 2
[2]
Trb. 3 Tb.
Cel.
rit.
a tempo
Vn. 1
Vn. 2
[div.]
[unis.]
Va.
[unis.]
Vc.
[div.]
Cb.

Florence Price

161
a 2
Fl. 1, 2
sf
mf
Ob. 1, 2
Cl. 1, 2 in A
[sf]
Bn. 1, 2
Hn. 1, 2 in F
[mp]
Hn. 3, 4 in F
Tpt. 1, 2 in A
[1]
p
Trb. 1, 2
[mf]
Trb. 3 Tb.
Cel.
[mf]
Vn. 1
pizz.
mp
Vn. 2
[mp]
Va.
Vc.
unis.
[div.]
pizz.
Cb.
[pizz.]

Florence Price

177
Fl. 1, 2
a 2
cantabile
mf
Ob. 1, 2
Cl. 1, 2
in A
Bn. 1, 2
Hn. 1, 2
in F
poco
mp
Hn. 3, 4
in F
poco
[mp]
Tpt. 1, 2
in A
1
pp
Trb. 1, 2
a
poco
mp
Trb. 3
Tb.
a
poco
mp
Cel.
Vn. 1
poco
mf
Vn. 2
poco
cantabile
mf
Va.
a
poco
div.
mp
Vc.
poco
[unis.]
mp
Cb.
poco
mp

Florence Price

187
Fl. 1, 2
Ob. 1, 2
Cl. 1, 2 in A
Bn. 1, 2
Hn. 1, 2 in F
Hn. 3, 4 in F
Tpt. 1, 2 in A
Trb. 1, 2
Trb. 3 Tb.
Cel.
Vn. 1
Vn. 2
Va.
Solo Vc.
Vc.
Cb.
[1]
[non div.]
[div.]
[unis.]
unis.
[col Tutti]
[unis.]
[div.]

Florence Price

198
Fl. 1, 2
Ob. 1, 2
Cl. 1, 2 in A
Bn. 1, 2
Hn. 1, 2 in F
Hn. 3, 4 in F
Tpt. 1, 2 in A
Trb. 1, 2
Trb. 3 Tb.
Timp.
Vn. 1
Vn. 2
Va.
Vc.
Cb.
cresc.
a 2
[1]
[cresc.]
[f]
mf
[mf]
tr
[non div.]
[unis.]
div.

Florence Price

209
Picc. 1, 2
[1]
f
Fl. 1, 2
[a 2]
f
Ob. 1, 2
Cl. 1, 2 in A
f
Bn. 1, 2
f
Hn. 1, 2 in F
Hn. 3, 4 in F
Tpt. 1, 2 in A
f
Trb. 1, 2
[1]
f
Trb. 3 Tb.
Vn. 1
f
Vn. 2
[f]
Va.
[unis.]
[f]
Vc.
div.
f
Cb.
[div.]
f

Florence Price

217
Picc. 1, 2
Fl. 1, 2
Ob. 1, 2
Cl. 1, 2 in A
Bn. 1, 2
Hn. 1, 2 in F
Hn. 3, 4 in F
Tpt. 1, 2 in A
Trb. 1, 2
Trb. 3 Tb.
Vn. 1
Vn. 2
Va.
Vc.
Cb.

221
Picc. 1, 2
Fl. 1, 2
Ob. 1, 2
Cl. 1, 2 in A
Bn. 1, 2
Hn. 1, 2 in F
Hn. 3, 4 in F
Tpt. 1, 2 in A
Trb. 1, 2
Trb. 3 Tb.
Trb. 3
Timp.
Vn. 1
Vn. 2
[non div.]
Va.
Vc.
[unis.]
Cb.
mf cresc.

227
[1]
rit.
Picc. 1, 2
[mf] [cresc.]
[a 2]
Fl. 1, 2
a 2
Ob. 1, 2
Cl. 1, 2 in A
[a 2]
Bn. 1, 2
Hn. 1, 2 in F
Hn. 3, 4 in F
Tpt. 1, 2 in A
[a 2]
Trb. 1, 2
Trb. 3 Tb.
tr
Timp.
rit.
8va
Vn. 1
Vn. 2
Va.
Vc.
Cb.

Florence Price

236
Picc. 1, 2
Fl. 1, 2
Ob. 1, 2
Cl. 1, 2 in A
Bn. 1, 2
[a 2]
p
Hn. 1, 2 in F
a 2
p
Hn. 3, 4 in F
Tpt. 1, 2 in A
mf
p
Trb. 1, 2
mf
p
Trb. 3 Tb.
[mf]
p
Timp.
tr
Cym. B. Dr.
Vn. 1
mf
p
Vn. 2
mf
[p]
Va.
div.
mf
p
unis.
Vc.
mf
Cb.

Florence Price

PLAY ONLY IF CUT IS MADE
OPTIONAL CUT
246
246b
Picc. 1, 2
Fl. 1, 2
Ob. 1, 2
Cl. 1, 2 in A
Bn. 1, 2
Hn. 1, 2 in F
Hn. 3, 4 in F
Tpt. 1, 2 in A
Trb. 1, 2
Trb. 3 Tb.
Timp.
Vn. 1
Vn. 2
Va.
Vc.
Cb.
[1]
[a 2]
[unis.]

Florence Price

257
rit.
a tempo
Picc. 1, 2
Fl. 1, 2
Ob. 1, 2
Cl. 1, 2 in A
Bn. 1, 2
Hn. 1, 2 in F
Hn. 3, 4 in F
Tpt. 1, 2 in A
Trb. 1, 2
Trb. 3 Tb.
Timp.
Vn. 1
Vn. 2
Va.
Vc.
Cb.
[div.]
[div.]
[arco]

Florence Price

270
più mosso
Picc. 1, 2
Fl. 1, 2
[a 2]
Ob. 1, 2
Cl. 1, 2 in A
Bn. 1, 2
Hn. 1, 2 in F
Hn. 3, 4 in F
Tpt. 1, 2 in A
Trb. 1, 2
Trb. 3 Tb.
Timp.
Trgl.
più mosso
Vn. 1
Vn. 2
Va.
Vc. 1
Vc. 2
Cb.
pizz.
arco
[unis.]
div.

276
Fl. 1, 2
Ob. 1, 2
Cl. 1, 2 in A
Bn. 1, 2
Hn. 1, 2 in F
Hn. 3, 4 in F
Tpt. 1, 2 in A
Trb. 1, 2
Trb. 3 Tb.
Timp.
B. Dr.
Vn. 1
Vn. 2
Va.
Vc.
Cb.
cresc.
[cresc.
mp cresc.
[a 2]
a 2
[1]
ff
[f]
[ff]
tr
unis.
[unis.]
div.

280
rit.
Fl. 1, 2
Ob. 1, 2
[a 2]
Cl. 1, 2 in A
Bn. 1, 2
Hn. 1, 2 in F
Hn. 3, 4 in F
Tpt. 1, 2 in A
Trb. 1, 2
[1]
Trb. 3 Tb.
Timp.
B. Dr.
Vn. 1
Vn. 2
[non div.]
Va.
Vc.
[div.]
[unis.]
Cb.
div.
unis.
cresc.
mp
mf
p
f

Florence Price

289
a tempo
accel.
Picc. 1, 2
Fl. 1, 2
Ob. 1, 2
Cl. 1, 2 in A
Bn. 1, 2
Hn. 1, 2 in F
Hn. 3, 4 in F
Tpt. 1, 2 in A
Trb. 1, 2
Trb. 3 Tb.
Timp.
Cym. B. Dr.
a tempo
accel.
Vn. 1
Vn. 2
Va.
[non div.]
Vc.
div.
Cb.

Florence Price

II

Largo, maestoso
Flute 1, 2
Oboe 1, 2
Clarinet 1, 2 in A
Bassoon 1, 2
Horn 1, 2 in F
Horn 3, 4 in F
Trumpet 1, 2 in A
Trombone 1, 2
Trombone 3 Tuba
Timpani
[Large] African Drum
Largo, maestoso
Violin 1
Violin 2
Viola
Violoncello
Contrabass

6
Fl. 1, 2
Cl. 1, 2 in A
Hn. 1, 2 in F
Hn. 3, 4 in F
Tpt. 1, 2 in A
Trb. 1, 2
Trb. 3 Tb.
Timp.
[Lg.] Afr.
mp
[1]
mf
cresc.
[mf]
[cresc.]
[mp]
mf cresc.
11
f
[f]
[p]
[mp]
[mf]
[mp] cresc.

16
Hn. 1, 2 in F
Hn. 3, 4 in F
Tpt. 1, 2 in A
Trb. 1, 2
Trb. 3 Tb.
Timp.
[Lg.] Afr.
mf
dim.
mp
[mf]
[dim.]
[mp]
21
p
[p]

Florence Price

37
Fl. 1, 2
Ob. 1, 2
Cl. 1, 2 in A
[1]
44
poco più mosso
Bn. 1, 2
Vn. 1
Vn. 2
49
Va.
Vc.
Cb.
[div.]

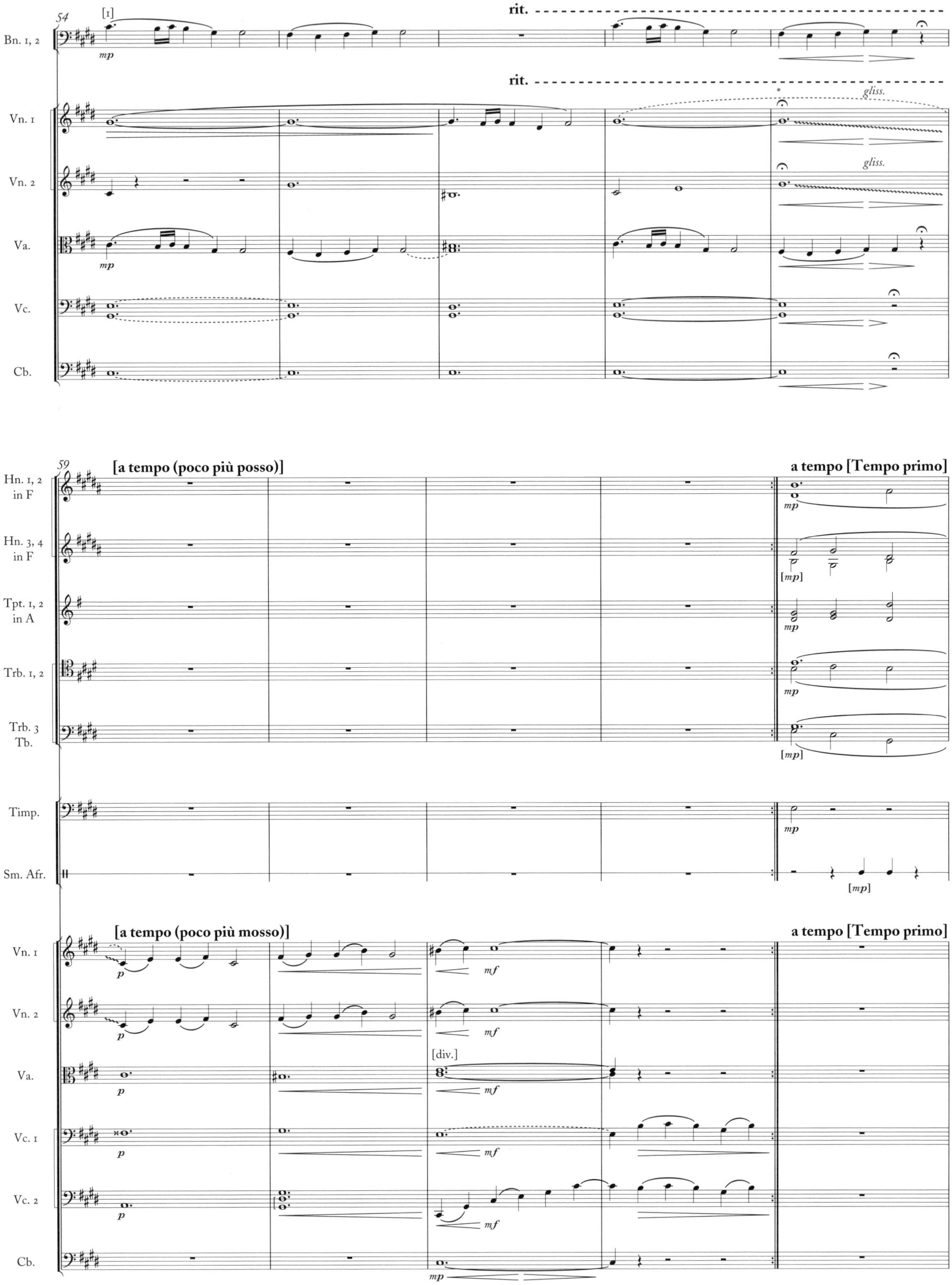

*The editor recommends 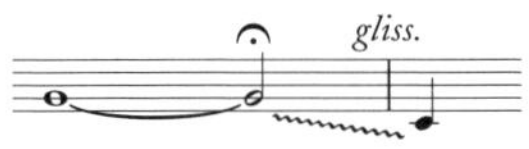

64
Fl. 1, 2
Ob. 1, 2
Cl. 1, 2 in A
Bn. 1, 2
Hn. 1, 2 in F
Hn. 3, 4 in F
Tpt. 1, 2 in A
Trb. 1, 2
Trb. 3 Tb.
Timp.
Sm. Afr.
Vn. 1
Vn. 2
Va.
Vc.
Cb.
p
[1]
mf
[mf]

70
Hn. 1, 2 in F
Hn. 3, 4 in F
Tpt. 1, 2 in A
Trb. 1, 2
Trb. 3 Tb.
Timp.
Sm. Afr.
75
Fl. 1, 2
Cl. 1, 2 in A
Hn. 1, 2 in F
Hn. 3, 4 in F
Tpt. 1, 2 in A
Trb. 1, 2
Trb. 3 Tb.
Timp.
Sm. Afr.
[Lg.] Afr.

80
poco rit.
Hn. 1, 2 in F
Hn. 3, 4 in F
Tpt. 1, 2 in A
Trb. 1, 2
Trb. 3 Tb.
Timp.
[Lg.] Afr.
mf
[mf]
f
[f]
85
a tempo
mp
[mp]

Florence Price

100
Fl. 1, 2
Ob. 1, 2
Cl. 1, 2 in A
Hn. 1, 2 in F
Hn. 3, 4 in F
Tpt. 1, 2 in A
Trb. 1, 2
Trb. 3 Tb.
cresc.
[a 2]
Trb. 3
[mf] [cresc.
[f]
[p]
105
Bn. 1, 2
Vn. 1
Vn. 2
Va.
Vc.
[div.] [mf]
unis.
div.

Florence Price

113
Fl. 1, 2
Ob. 1, 2
Cl. 1, 2 in A
Bn. 1, 2
Hn. 1, 2 in F
Hn. 3, 4 in F
Tpt. 1, 2 in A
Trb. 1, 2
Trb. 3 Tb.
Vn. 1
Vn. 2
Va.
Vc.
Cb.
1
a 2
mp
f
[f]
[mp]
[1]
p
[non div.]
div.
unis.
[p]

118
rit.
a tempo
a 2
[a 2]
Fl. 1, 2
Ob. 1, 2
Cl. 1, 2 in A
Bn. 1, 2
Hn. 1, 2 in F
Hn. 3, 4 in F
Tpt. 1, 2 in A
Trb. 1, 2
Trb. 3 Tb.
[non div.]
div.
unis.
[div.]
[unis.]
Vn. 1
Vn. 2
Va.
Vc. 1
Vc. 2
Cb.
p
[p]
mp
mf
f
[cresc.]
mp cresc.
[mp] [cresc.]
p [cresc.]
[p] [cresc.]

124
Fl. 1, 2
Ob. 1, 2
Cl. 1, 2 in A
Bn. 1, 2
Hn. 1, 2 in F
Hn. 3, 4 in F
Tpt. 1, 2 in A
Trb. 1, 2
Trb. 3 Tb.
Vn. 1
Vn. 2
Va. 1
Va. 2
Vc.
Cb.
[a 2]
[non div.]
div.
[div.]
tr

Florence Price

135
a tempo
accel.
a tempo
Fl. 1, 2
Ob. 1, 2
Cl. 1, 2
in A
Bn. 1, 2
Trb. 1, 2
Trb. 3
Tb.
Vn. 1
Vn. 2
Va.
Vc. 1
Vc. 2
p
mp cresc.
f
mp
[p]
[mp] [cresc.]
[f]
pizz.
unis.
[non div.]
141
div.
arco
pizz.
pp
[mp]
mf
[mf]
[arco]
[cresc.

Florence Price

159
Ob. 1, 2
Cl. 1, 2 in A
Bn. 1, 2
Hn. 1, 2 in F
Hn. 3, 4 in F
Trb. 1, 2
Trb. 3 Tb.
Vn. 1
Vn. 2
rit.
a 2
mp
[mp]
p
164
a tempo
[a 2]
mf
[p]
[unis.]
[div.]
Va.
Vc.
Cb.
3

Florence Price

175
Fl. 1, 2
Ob. 1, 2
Cl. 1, 2 in A
Bn. 1, 2
Hn. 1, 2 in F
Hn. 3, 4 in F
Trb. 1, 2
Trb. 3 Tb.
[1]
[p]
più moss[o]
[a 2]
pp
3
p
[p]
1
181
Tpt. 1, 2 in A

Florence Price

[più mosso]
192
Fl. 1, 2
Ob. 1, 2
Cl. 1, 2 in A
Bn. 1, 2
Hn. 1, 2 in F
Hn. 3, 4 in F
Tpt. 1, 2 in A
Trb. 1, 2
Trb. 3 Tb.
Timp.
[Lg.] Afr.
[più mosso]
Vn. 1
Vn. 2
Va.
Vc.
[div.]
Cb.

Florence Price

204
Fl. 1, 2
Ob. 1, 2
Cl. 1, 2 in A
Bn. 1, 2
Vn. 1
Vn. 2
Va.
Vc.
Cb.
[a 2]
tr
mp
f
[f]
210
Tempo primo
Fl. 1, 2
Cl. 1, 2 in A
Hn. 1, 2 in F
Hn. 3, 4 in F
Tpt. 1, 2 in A
Trb. 1, 2
Trb. 3 Tb.
mf
[mp]

Florence Price

220
Fl. 1, 2
Cl. 1, 2 in A
Bn. 1, 2
Hn. 1, 2 in F
Hn. 3, 4 in F
Tpt. 1, 2 in A
Trb. 1, 2
Trb. 3 Tb.
Bells
mp
[p]
p
[a 2]
[mp]
mp
223
mf
[mf]

Florence Price

232
Cl. 1, 2 in A
Hn. 1, 2 in F
Hn. 3, 4 in F
Tpt. 1, 2 in A
Trb. 1, 2
Trb. 3 Tb.
Cath. Ch.
mp
[mp]
8va
235
[pp]
pp
mf

Florence Price

245
Fl. 1, 2
Ob. 1, 2
Cl. 1, 2 in A
Bn. 1, 2
Hn. 1, 2 in F
Hn. 3, 4 in F
Cath. Ch.
Bells
mp
f
[mp]
[f]
248
Trb. 1, 2
Trb. 3 Tb.
[2]

251
a 2
poco rit.
[a tempo]
Marcando
Fl. 1, 2
p
dim.
ff
Ob. 1, 2
[p]
Cl. 1, 2
in A
[a 2]
Bn. 1, 2
[dim.]
Hn. 1, 2
in F
Hn. 3, 4
in F
[ff]
Tpt. 1, 2
in A
Trb. 1, 2
p dim.
Trb. 3
Tb.
p dim.
Timp.
tr
Sm. Afr.
[Lg.] Afr.
[tr]
Bells
Vn. 1
Vn. 2
Va. 1
Va. 2
[div.]
Vc.
Cb.

255
Fl. 1, 2
Ob. 1, 2
Cl. 1, 2 in A
Bn. 1, 2
Hn. 1, 2 in F
Hn. 3, 4 in F
Tpt. 1, 2 in A
Trb. 1, 2
Trb. 3 Tb.
Timp.
Sm. Afr.
[Lg.] Afr.
Bells
Vn. 1
Vn. 2
Va. 1
Va. 2
Vc.
Cb.
mf
dim.
[pp]
a 2
pp
[a 2]
[mf]
[dim.]
tr
[tr]
mp
unis.
div.
[ff]

Florence Price

III. JUBA DANCE

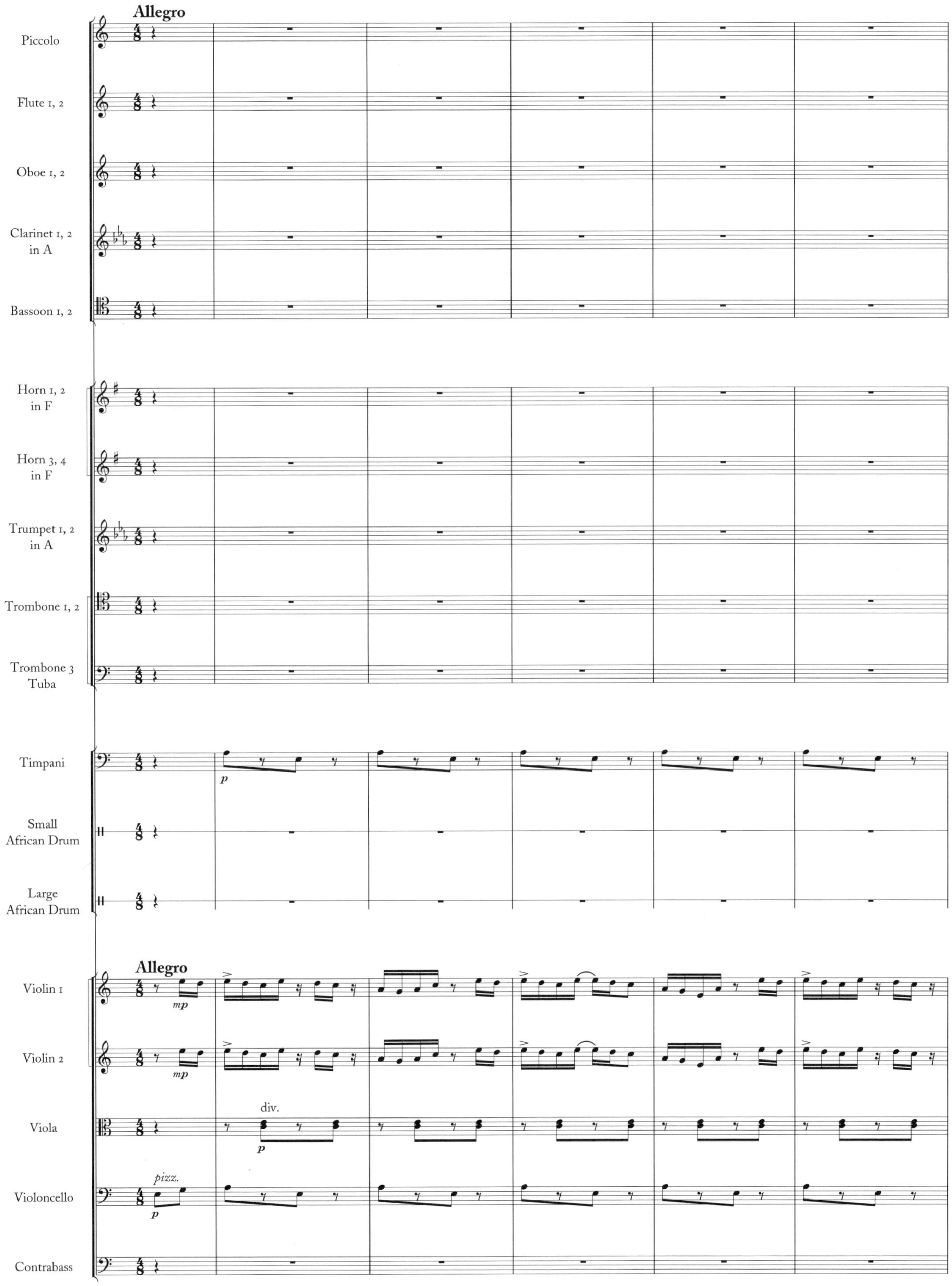

Florence Price

18
Fl. 1, 2
Ob. 1, 2
Cl. 1, 2 in A
Bn. 1, 2
Hn. 1, 2 in F
Hn. 3, 4 in F
Tpt. 1, 2 in A
Trb. 1, 2
Trb. 3 Tb.
Sm. Afr.
Lg. Afr.
Cr. Cym.
short crash
mf
Vn. 1
Vn. 2
Va.
[div.]
Vc.
Cb.

Florence Price

36
Bn. 1, 2
[a 2]
[mf]
Timp.
[mf]
Sm. Afr.
Lg. Afr.
W. Wh.
Vn. 1
Vn. 2
Va.
[non div.]
Vc.
Cb.
42
Ob. 1, 2
[a 2]
[mf]
mp
Bn. 1, 2
mp
Timp.
mp
Sm. Afr.
mp
mp
Lg. Afr.
mp
Vn. 1
mp
Vn. 2
mp
Va.
mp
Vc.
mp
Cb.

Florence Price

61
Fl. 1, 2
Ob. 1, 2
Cl. 1, 2
in A
[a 2]
Bn. 1, 2
[a 2]
Hn. 1, 2
in F
Hn. 3, 4
in F
Tpt. 1, 2
in A
Trb. 1, 2
Trb. 3
Tb.
Timp.
tr
[f]
Sm. Afr.
Lg. Afr.
Vn. 1
Vn. 2
[f]
Va.
[div.]
Vc.
Cb.

Florence Price

73
Fl. 1, 2
Ob. 1, 2
Cl. 1, 2 in A
Bn. 1, 2
Hn. 1, 2 in F
Hn. 3, 4 in F
Tpt. 1, 2 in A
Trb. 1, 2
Trb. 3 Tb.
Timp.
Sm. Afr.
Lg. Afr.
Vn. 1
Vn. 2
Va.
Vc.
Cb.
div.

*Ossia: tacet mm. 81–96. See Critical Commentary.

Florence Price

86
Hn. 1, 2 in F
Hn. 3, 4 in F
Trb. 1, 2
Trb. 3 Tb.
Timp.
Sn. Dr.
cresc.
mf
dim.
p
[p]
[cresc.]
[mf]
[dim.]
93
Fl. 1, 2
Ob. 1, 2
Cl. 1, 2 in A
Bn. 1, 2
Hn. 1, 2 in F
Hn. 3, 4 in F
Trb. 1, 2
Trb. 3 Tb.
Timp.
Sn. Dr. Sm. Afr.
Lg. Afr.
[a 2]
mf
mp
[mp]
[mf]

Florence Price

108
rit.
a tempo
Fl. 1, 2
a 2
mf
Ob. 1, 2
Cl. 1, 2
in A
[mf]
2
Bn. 1, 2
Hn. 1, 2
in F
f
mp
mf
Hn. 3, 4
in F
[mf]
Trb. 1, 2
[1]
[mf]
Trb. 3
Tb.
[f]
[mp]
Sm. Afr.
Lg. Afr.
Vn. 1
Vn. 2
Va.
div.
Vc.
[div.]
Cb.

Florence Price

123
Fl. 1, 2
Ob. 1, 2
Cl. 1, 2 in A
Bn. 1, 2
[a 2]
Hn. 1, 2 in F
Hn. 3, 4 in F
Tpt. 1, 2 in A
Trb. 1, 2
Trb. 3 Tb.
Sm. Afr.
Lg. Afr.
Vn. 1
Vn. 2
Va.
Vc.
Cb.
ff
[ff]

Florence Price

135
Fl. 1, 2
Ob. 1, 2
Cl. 1, 2 in A
Bn. 1, 2
[a 2]
Hn. 1, 2 in F
Hn. 3, 4 in F
Tpt. 1, 2 in A
Trb. 1, 2
Trb. 3 Tb.
Sm. Afr.
Lg. Afr.
Vn. 1
Vn. 2
Va.
Vc.
Cb.
[div.]
[unis.]

Florence Price

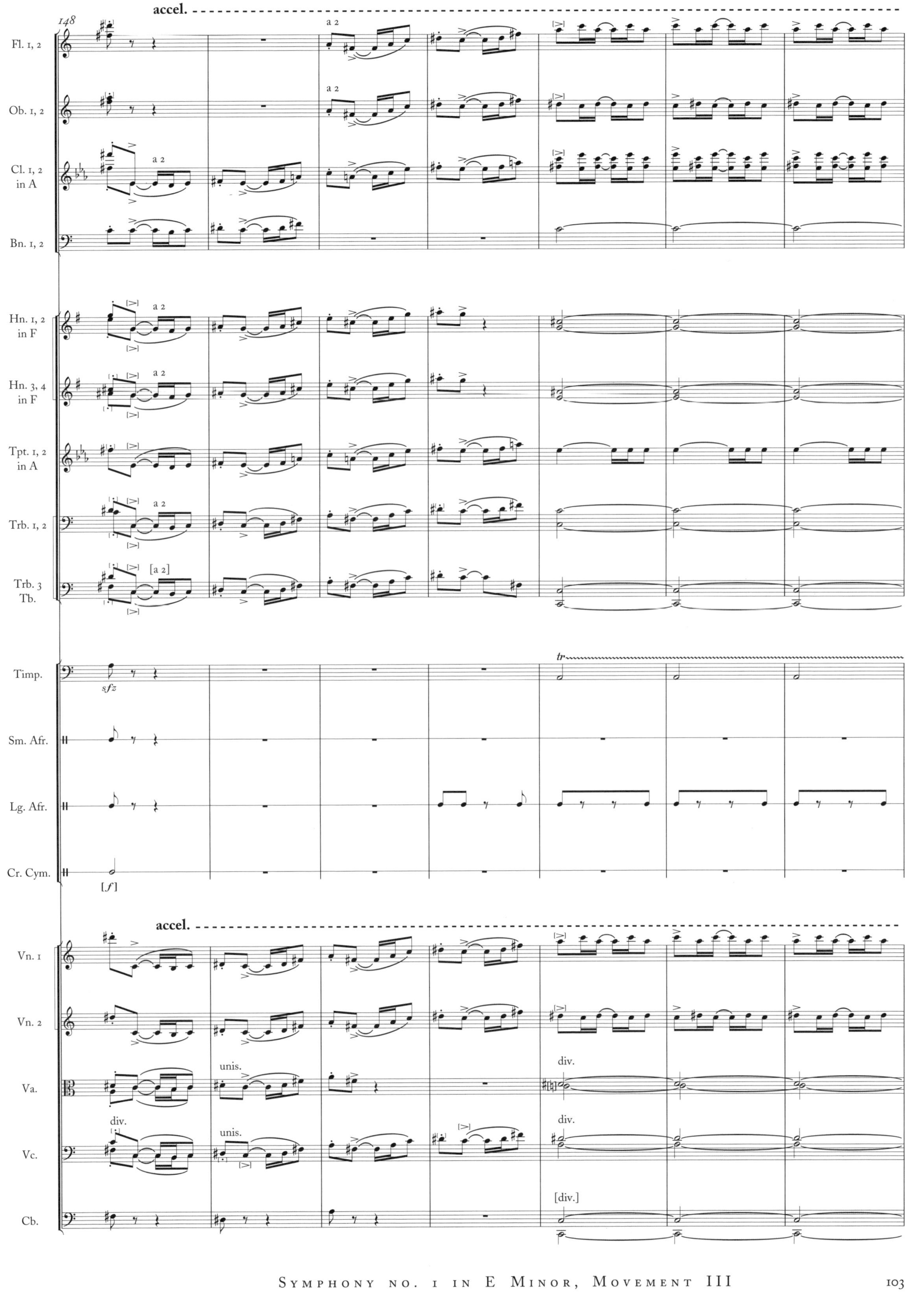
accel.
148
Fl. 1, 2
Ob. 1, 2
Cl. 1, 2 in A
Bn. 1, 2
Hn. 1, 2 in F
Hn. 3, 4 in F
Tpt. 1, 2 in A
Trb. 1, 2
Trb. 3 Tb.
Timp.
Sm. Afr.
Lg. Afr.
Cr. Cym.
Vn. 1
Vn. 2
Va.
Vc.
Cb.
a 2
[a 2]
sfz
[f]
tr
unis.
div.
[div.]

Florence Price

163
Picc.
Fl. 1, 2
Ob. 1, 2
Cl. 1, 2 in A
a 2
Bn. 1, 2
[a 2]
Hn. 1, 2 in F
a 2
Hn. 3, 4 in F
[a 2]
Tpt. 1, 2 in A
Trb. 1, 2
a 2
p
Trb. 3 Tb.
a 2
[p]
Timp.
[p]
Sm. Afr.
Lg. Afr.
Cr. Cym.
Vn. 1
p
Vn. 2
[p]
Va.
unis.
[p]
Vc.
div.
[p]
Cb.
[p]

Florence Price

181
Picc.
Fl. 1, 2
Ob. 1, 2
Cl. 1, 2 in A
Bn. 1, 2
Hn. 1, 2 in F
Hn. 3, 4 in F
Tpt. 1, 2 in A
Trb. 1, 2
Trb. 3 Tb.
Timp.
Sn. Dr.
B. Dr.
Cr. Cym.
Vn. 1
Vn. 2
Va.
Vc.
Cb.
[ff]
[ffz]
ffz
[a 2]
tr
[ff]
div.

IV. FINALE

Florence Price

7
Picc.
Fl. 1, 2
Ob. 1, 2
Cl. 1, 2 in A
Bn. 1, 2
Hn. 1, 2 in F
Hn. 3, 4 in F
Tpt. 1, 2 in A
Trb. 1, 2
Trb. 3 Tb.
Timp.
Cym.
Vn. 1
Vn. 2
Va.
Vc.
Cb.
a 2
ff
[ff]
tr
non div.
div.

Florence Price

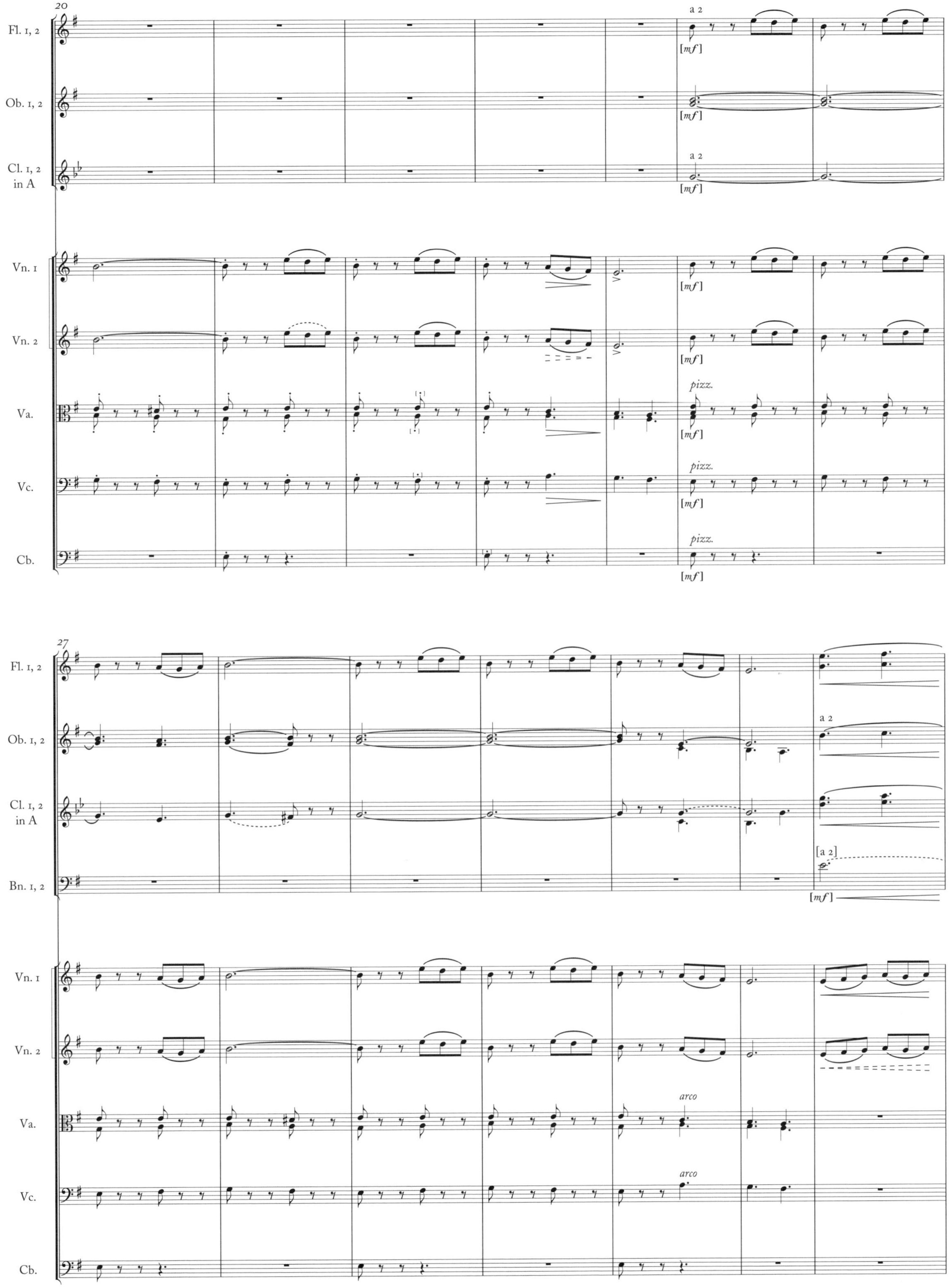
20
Fl. 1, 2
Ob. 1, 2
Cl. 1, 2 in A
Vn. 1
Vn. 2
Va.
Vc.
Cb.
a 2
[mf]
pizz.
27
Bn. 1, 2
[a 2]
arco

Florence Price

49
Fl. 1, 2
Ob. 1, 2
Cl. 1, 2
in A
Bn. 1, 2
[a 2]
Hn. 1, 2
in F
Hn. 3, 4
in F
Trb. 1, 2
Trb. 3
Tb.
Timp.
Vn. 1
Vn. 2
Va.
Vc.
Cb.
1.
pizz.
arco
div.
[div.]
f
[f]
mp
[mp]

(56b)
2.
Fl. 1, 2
Ob. 1, 2
Cl. 1, 2 in A
Bn. 1, 2
[a 2]
Hn. 1, 2 in F
Hn. 3, 4 in F
Trb. 1, 2
Trb. 3 Tb.
Timp.
Vn. 1
Vn. 2
Va.
unis.
Vc.
Cb.
[div.]
[mp] dim.
[mp][dim.]
p cresc.
mp
dim.
p
cresc.
mf
[p]
[mp]
[cresc.]
[mf]

64
[a 2]
Ob. 1, 2
Cl. 1, 2
in A
Trb. 1, 2
Trb. 3
Tb.
Timp.
Vn. 1
Vn. 2
Va.
Vc.
Cb.
71
Bn. 1, 2
div.
unis.

Florence Price

103
poco rit. - - - - a tempo
Cl. 1, 2 in A
a 2
Hn. 1, 2 in F
Hn. 3, 4 in F
Trb. 1, 2
Trb. 3 Tb.
Vn. 1
pizz.
Vn. 2
Va.
[div.]
unis.
Vc.
[arco]
Cb.
arco
111

119
Fl. 1, 2
Ob. 1, 2
Bn. 1, 2
Hn. 1, 2 in F
Vn. 1
Vn. 2
Va.
Vc.
Cb.
[a 2]
arco
[arco]
div.
unis.
pizz.
[pizz.]
cresc.
[cresc.]
127

135
Vn. 1
Vn. 2
Va.
Vc.
Cb.
unis.
arco
mf
[mf]
[div.]
[mf]
143
[1]
Tpt. 1, 2
in A
pp cresc. poco a poco [p]
p
[p]
div.
unis.
151
[a 2]
Fl. 1, 2
p

Florence Price

173
Fl. 1, 2
Ob. 1, 2
a 2
Cl. 1, 2 in A
a 2
Bn. 1, 2
Hn. 1, 2 in F
Hn. 3, 4 in F
Tpt. 1, 2 in A
Trb. 1, 2
Trb. 3 Tb.
Timp.
Vn. 1
Vn. 2
Va.
non div.
div.
Vc.
non div.
Cb.

Florence Price

187
Fl. 1, 2
Ob. 1, 2
Cl. 1, 2 in A
[a 2]
Bn. 1, 2
Trb. 1, 2
Trb. 3 Tb.
Timp.
Vn. 1
Vn. 2
Va.
Vc.
Cb.
f
[f]
dim.
[dim.
194
p
[p]
cresc.
[cresc.
unis.
[>]

Florence Price

212
Fl. 1, 2
a 2
mf cresc.
Ob. 1, 2
Cl. 1, 2 in A
mp
cresc.
Bn. 1, 2
Hn. 1, 2 in F
mp cresc.
Hn. 3, 4 in F
[mp] [cresc]
Trb. 1, 2
Trb. 3 Tb.
[mp] [cresc.]
Timp.
Vn. 1
Vn. 2
Va.
Vc.
div.
Cb.

Florence Price

225
Fl. 1, 2
Ob. 1, 2
a 2
[ff]
Cl. 1, 2 in A
Bn. 1, 2
Hn. 1, 2 in F
Hn. 3, 4 in F
Trb. 1, 2
Trb. 3 Tb.
Timp.
Vn. 1
Vn. 2
Va.
div.
Vc.
Cb.
unis.

Florence Price

239
Fl. 1, 2
Ob. 1, 2
Cl. 1, 2 in A
Bn. 1, 2
Trb. 1, 2
Trb. 3 Tb.
Timp.
Vn. 1
Vn. 2
Va.
Vc.
Cb.
mp
[mp]
[div.]
246
[a 2]

Florence Price

267
rit.
a tempo [Tempo primo]
poco meno moso
Fl. 1, 2
a 2
Ob. 1, 2
Cl. 1, 2 in A
Timp.
a tempo [Tempo primo]
poco meno mosso
Vn. 1
Vn. 2
unis.
div.
Va.
unis.
Vc.
Cb.
274
Cl. 1, 2 in A
rit.
Tempo primo
Timp.
Vn. 1
Vn. 2
Va.
Vc.
Cb.

Florence Price

288
molto rit.
Picc.
Fl. 1, 2
Ob. 1, 2
a 2
Cl. 1, 2 in A
mf cresc.
Bn. 1, 2
Hn. 1, 2 in F
Hn. 3, 4 in F
Tpt. 1, 2 in A
Trb. 1, 2
Trb. 3 Tb.
Timp.
molto rit.
Vn. 1
Vn. 2
Va.
div.
unis.
div.
unis.
Vc.
div.
Cb.
[div.]

295
Prestissimo
a 2
Fl. 1, 2
Ob. 1, 2
Cl. 1, 2 in A
Bn. 1, 2
Hn. 1, 2 in F
Hn. 3, 4 in F
Tpt. 1, 2 in A
[a 2]
Trb. 1, 2
Trb. 3 Tb.
Timp.
Cym.
B. Dr. Lg. Afr.
Vn. 1
Vn. 2
Va.
Vc.
Cb.
cresc.
[cresc.
[f]
[ff]

302
Fl. 1, 2
Ob. 1, 2
Cl. 1, 2 in A
Bn. 1, 2
ff
Hn. 1, 2 in F
Hn. 3, 4 in F
Tpt. 1, 2 in A
Trb. 1, 2
ff
[a 2]
Trb. 3 Tb.
[ff]
Trb. 3
Timp.
Cym.
B. Dr. Lg. Afr.
Vn. 1
Vn. 2
Va.
ff
Vc.
ff
div.
unis.
Cb.
[unis.]
ff

Florence Price

316
Picc.
Fl. 1, 2
Ob. 1, 2
Cl. 1, 2 in A
Bn. 1, 2
Hn. 1, 2 in F
Hn. 3, 4 in F
Tpt. 1, 2 in A
Trb. 1, 2
Trb. 3 Tb.
Timp.
Cym.
B. Dr. Lg. Afr.
Vn. 1
Vn. 2
Va.
Vc.
Cb.
[ff]
8va
ff cresc.
fffz
[ff] [cresc.]
[fffz]
tr
plate roll
crash
ff
div.
unis.
[non div.]

SYMPHONY NO. 3 IN C MINOR

INSTRUMENTS

Piccolo
Flute 1, 2, 3
Oboe, 1, 2
English Horn
Clarinet 1, 2 in B♭, A
Bass Clarinet in B♭
Bassoon 1, 2

Horn 1, 2, 3, 4 in F
Trumpet 1, 2, 3 in B♭, A
Trombone 1, 2, 3
Tuba

Timpani
Percussion (Tambourine, Snare Drum, Cymbal, Bass Drum, Triangle, Crash Cymbals, Wood Block, Sand Paper, Castanets, Slapstick, Gong, Orchestral Bells, Xylophone)

Celesta
Harp

Violin 1, 2
Viola
Violoncello
Contrabass

I

Andante
rit.
Piccolo
Flute 1, 2
Flute 3
Oboe 1, 2
English Horn
Clarinet 1, 2 in B♭
Bass Clarinet in B♭
Bassoon 1, 2
Horn 1, 2 in F
Horn 3, 4 in F
Trumpet 1, 2 in B♭
Trumpet 3 in B♭
Trombone 1, 2
Trombone 3
Tuba
Timpani
Snare Drum
Orchestral Bells
Harp
Andante
rit.
Violin 1
Violin 2
Viola
Violoncello
Contrabass
mp
mf
cresc.
[mp] cresc.
[mf]
p
[mf]
pp

Florence Price

poco rit.
a tempo
poco rit.
Allegro
Fl. 1, 2
Fl. 3
Ob. 1, 2
E. Hn.
Cl. 1, 2 in B♭
Bn. 1, 2
Hn. 1, 2 in F
Hn. 3, 4 in F
Tpt. 1, 2 in B♭
Tpt. 3 in B♭
Trb. 1, 2
Trb. 3
Tb.
Timp.
Bells
Hp.
Va.
Vc.
Cb.
scen do
pizz.
pizz.

Florence Price

29
[a 2]
Fl. 1, 2
Fl. 3
Ob. 1, 2
E. Hn.
Cl. 1, 2 in B♭
B. Cl. in B♭
Bn. 1, 2
Hn. 1, 2 in F
Tpt. 1, 2 in B♭
Tpt. 3 in B♭
Trb. 1, 2
Trb. 3 Tb.
Timp.
Sn. Dr.
Cym. B. Dr.
Hp.
Vn. 1
Vn. 2
Va.
Vc.
Cb.
f marc.
[f] [marc.]
[a 2]
a 2
[marc.]
[div.]
[unis.]
pizz.

36
Fl. 1, 2
Fl. 3
Ob. 1, 2
E. Hn.
Cl. 1, 2 in B♭
B. Cl. in B♭
Bn. 1, 2
Tpt. 1, 2 in B♭
Tpt. 3 in B♭
Trb. 1, 2
Trb. 3 Tb.
Timp.
Sn. Dr.
Cym. B. Dr.
Hp.
Vn. 1
Vn. 2
Va.
Vc.
Cb.
[a 2]
a 2
mp tranquillo
mf tranquillo
[div.]
[unis.]

41
Fl. 1, 2
Fl. 3
Ob. 1, 2
E. Hn.
Cl. 1, 2 in B♭
B. Cl. in B♭
Bn. 1, 2
Tpt. 1, 2 in B♭
Tpt. 3 in B♭
Trb. 1, 2
Trb. 3 Tb.
Timp.
Sn. Dr.
Cym. B. Dr.
Hp.
Vn. 1
Vn. 2
Va.
Vc.
Cb.
pp cresc.
mf
[mf]
p
cresc.
espress.
mp tranquillo
solo
p tranquillo
[p] [cresc.
][mf]
(ossia: con sordino)
[div.]

Florence Price

55
Picc.
Fl. 1, 2
Fl. 3
Ob. 1, 2
E. Hn.
Cl. 1, 2 in B♭
Tpt. 1, 2 in B♭
Tpt. 3 in B♭
Trb. 1, 2
Trb. 3 Tb.
Timp.
Sn. Dr.
Cym. B. Dr.
Hp.
Vn. 1
Vn. 2
Va.
Solo Vc.
Vc.
Cb.
[a 2]
[div.]
[unis.]
[non div.]
[senza sordino]
[div. in 3]
[div. in 2]
[col Tutti]
cresc.
[pp] cresc.
mp
sf
[sf]
f
[f]
p
tr

61
Picc.
Fl. 1, 2
Fl. 3
Ob. 1, 2
E. Hn.
Cl. 1, 2 in B♭
B. Cl. in B♭
Bn. 1, 2
Hn. 1, 2 in F
Hn. 3, 4 in F
Tpt. 1, 2 in B♭
Tpt. 3 in B♭
Trb. 1, 2
Trb. 3 Tb.
Timp.
Sn. Dr.
Cym. B. Dr.
Hp.
Vn. 1
Vn. 2
Va.
Vc.
Cb.
[a 2]
a 2
[unis.]
mf
[mf]
[m]f
f
[f]
ff
[ff]
tr

66
accel.
Picc.
Fl. 1, 2
Fl. 3
Ob. 1, 2
E. Hn.
Cl. 1, 2 in B♭
B. Cl. in B♭
Bn. 1, 2
Hn. 1, 2 in F
Hn. 3, 4 in F
Tpt. 1, 2 in B♭
Tpt. 3 in B♭
Trb. 1, 2
Trb. 3 Tb.
Timp.
Sn. Dr.
Cym. B. Dr.
Hp.
accel.
Vn. 1
Vn. 2
Va.
Vc.
Cb.
[a 2]
[div.]
[unis.]
8va

Florence Price

76
meno mosso
Picc.
Fl. 1, 2
Fl. 3
Ob. 1, 2
E. Hn.
Cl. 1, 2 in B♭
a 2
1
mp
p cresc.
pp
B. Cl. in B♭
Bn. 1, 2
mp
Hn. 1, 2 in F
cresc.
pp
Hn. 3, 4 in F
[mp] [cresc.
]
[pp]
Tpt. 1, 2 in B♭
p
pp cresc.
p
Tpt. 3 in B♭
[p]
[pp]
[p]
Trb. 1
solo
mf cresc.
f
Trb. 2
pp cresc.
Trb. 3 Tb.
pp cresc.
mp
Hp.
p
[mp]
meno mosso
Vn. 1
p
cresc.
pp [cresc.
]
mp
Vn. 2
[p]
[cresc.
]
[pp] [cresc.
]
[mp]
Va.
Vc.
p
cresc.
pp cresc.
mp
Cb.
pp cresc.
mp

Florence Price

89
rit.
a tempo
Picc.
Fl. 1, 2
mp
Ob. 1, 2
mp espress.
[mp]
Cl. 1, 2 in B♭
Bn. 1, 2
Tpt. 1, 2 in B♭
Tpt. 3 in B♭
Trb. 1
mf
Trb. 2
Trb. 3 Tb.
Bells
Hp.
Vn. 1
espress.
Vn. 2
[mf]
Va.
[div.]
[unis.]
Vc.
Cb.

Florence Price

102
Picc.
Fl. 1, 2
Fl. 3
Ob. 1, 2
E. Hn.
Cl. 1, 2 in B♭
B. Cl. in B♭
Bn. 1, 2
Hn. 1, 2 in F
Hn. 3, 4 in F
Tpt. 1, 2 in B♭
Tpt. 3 in B♭
Trb. 1
Trb. 2
Trb. 3 Tb.
Timp.
Sn. Dr.
Cym. B. Dr.
Hp.
Vn. 1
Vn. 2
Va.
Vc.
Cb.
[a 2]
[div.]
[unis.]
espress.

108
poco rit.
a tempo
poco accel.
Picc.
Fl. 1, 2
Fl. 3
Ob. 1, 2
E. Hn.
Cl. 1, 2 in B♭
B. Cl. in B♭
Bn. 1, 2
Hn. 1, 2 in F
Hn. 3, 4 in F
Tpt. 1, 2 in B♭
Tpt. 3 in B♭
Trb. 1
Trb. 2
Trb. 3 Tb.
Timp.
Sn. Dr.
Bells
Hp.
Vn. 1
Vn. 2
Va.
Vc.
Cb.
[a 2]
dim.
mp
espress.
cresc.

115
a tempo
poco rit.
[a tempo]
Picc.
Fl. 1, 2
solo
Fl. 3
Ob. 1, 2
E. Hn.
Cl. 1, 2 in B♭
1
pp espress.
B. Cl. in B♭
Bn. 1, 2
[pp]
Hn. 1, 2 in F
Hn. 3, 4 in F
Tpt. 1, 2 in B♭
Tpt. 3 in B♭
Trb. 1
Trb. 2
Trb. 3 Tb.
Timp.
tr
Sn. Dr.
Bells
Hp.
a tempo
poco rit.
[a tempo]
espress.
sur la touche
Vn. 1
p cresc.
[espress.
[sur la touche]
Vn. 2
[mf]
[pp]
[p] [cresc.]
[unis.]
[sur la touche]
Va.
p cresc.
[sur la touche]
Vc.
p cresc.
Cb.

Florence Price

129
poco rit.
Tempo I
Picc.
Fl. 1, 2
[a 2]
Fl. 3
Ob. 1, 2
[1]
E. Hn.
[p]
Cl. 1, 2 in B♭
[p]
Bn. 1, 2
Trgl.
Bells
Hp.
poco rit.
Tempo I
Vn. 1
Vn. 2
[mf]
Va.
pizz.
Vc.
pizz.
arco
Cb.
pizz.

Florence Price

141
Picc.
Fl. 1, 2
Fl. 3
Ob. 1, 2
E. Hn.
Cl. 1, 2 in B♭
B. Cl. in B♭
Bn. 1, 2
Hn. 1, 2 in F
Hn. 3, 4 in F
Tpt. 1, 2 in B♭
Tpt. 3 in B♭
Trb. 1, 2
Trb. 3 Tb.
Timp.
Sn. Dr.
Cym. B. Dr.
Vn. 1
Vn. 2
Va.
Vc.
Cb.
mf
cresc.
f
[mf]
[cresc.]
[f]
[a 2]
tr
[unis.]
[div.]

Florence Price

151
a tempo
accel.
Picc.
Fl. 1, 2
Fl. 3
Ob. 1, 2
E. Hn.
Cl. 1, 2 in B♭
B. Cl. in B♭
Bn. 1, 2
Hn. 1, 2 in F
Hn. 3, 4 in F
Tpt. 1, 2 in B♭
Tpt. 3 in B♭
Trb. 1, 2
Trb. 3 Tb.
Timp.
Tamb. Sn. Dr.
Cym. B. Dr.
Vn. 1
Vn. 2
Va.
Vc.
Cb.
[a 2]
[div.]
[unis.]
mf cre- scen- do
[mf] [cre scen- do
[f] [cresc.
cresc.
mp

157
a tempo
poco rit.
Picc.
[a 2]
Fl. 1, 2
Fl. 3
Ob. 1, 2
E. Hn.
Cl. 1, 2 in B♭
B. Cl. in B♭
Bn. 1, 2
Hn. 1, 2 in F
Hn. 3, 4 in F
Tpt. 1, 2 in B♭
Tpt. 3 in B♭
Trb. 1, 2
Trb. 3 Tb.
Timp.
Tamb. Sn. Dr.
Cym. B. Dr.
Trgl.
Vn. 1
Vn. 2
Va.
Vc.
Cb.
dim.
[dim.
[unis.]
[div.]
[div.]

162
a tempo
rit.
Picc.
Fl. 1, 2
Fl. 3
Ob. 1, 2
E. Hn.
Cl. 1, 2 in B♭
B. Cl. in B♭
Bn. 1, 2
Hn. 1, 2 in F
Hn. 3, 4 in F
Tpt. 1, 2 in B♭
Tpt. 3 in B♭
Trb. 1, 2
Trb. 3 Tb.
Timp.
Tamb. Sn. Dr.
Cym. B. Dr.
Trgl.
Vn. 1
Vn. 2
Va.
Vc.
Cb.
mp cresc.
mp
cresc.
[mp] cresc.
mf
f
[mf]
[f]
tr
dim.
[dim.

168
a tempo
Fl. 1, 2
Fl. 3
Ob. 1, 2
E. Hn.
Cl. 1, 2 in B♭
Bn. 1, 2
Vn. 1
Vn. 2
Va.
Vc.
Cb.
173
[div.]
[unis.]
[div.]
[unis.]

179
Picc.
Fl. 1, 2
Fl. 3
Ob. 1, 2
E. Hn.
Cl. 1, 2 in B♭
B. Cl. in B♭
Bn. 1, 2
Hn. 1, 2 in F
Hn. 3, 4 in F
Tpt. 1, 2 in B♭
Tpt. 3 in B♭
Trb. 1, 2
Trb. 3 Tb.
Tamb. Sn. Dr.
Cym. B. Dr.
Vn. 1
Vn. 2
Va.
Vc.
Cb.
[a 2]
[1]
a 2
[a 2]
a 2
tr
div.
[unis.]
[div.]
[unis.]
[div.]
[unis.]
[div.]
[div.]
[unis.]
[div.]
[unis.]
ff
mf
[mf]
[ff]
sf

185
poco accel.
a tempo
Picc.
Fl. 1, 2
Fl. 3
Ob. 1, 2
E. Hn.
Cl. 1, 2 in B♭
B. Cl. in B♭
Bn. 1, 2
Hn. 1, 2 in F
Hn. 3, 4 in F
Tpt. 1, 2 in B♭
Tpt. 3 in B♭
Trb. 1, 2
Trb. 3 Tb.
Timp.
Sn. Dr.
Cym. B. Dr.
Hp.
Vn. 1
Vn. 2
Va.
Vc.
Cb.
[a 2]
a 2
[1]
[div.]
[unis.]
f
[f]
mf
[mf]
mp
[mp]

190
poco rit.
a tempo
poco meno mosso
Picc.
Fl. 1, 2
Fl. 3
Ob. 1, 2
E. Hn.
Cl. 1, 2 in B♭
B. Cl. in B♭
Bn. 1, 2
Hn. 1, 2 in F
Hn. 3, 4 in F
Tpt. 1, 2 in B♭
Tpt. 3 in B♭
Trb. 1, 2
Trb. 3 Tb.
Timp.
Sn. Dr.
Cym. B. Dr.
Hp.
Vn. 1
Vn. 2
Va.
Vc.
Cb.
[1]
[a 2]
[espress.]
cresc.
[cresc.]
[unis.]
espress.
div.

Florence Price

199
Picc.
Fl. 1, 2
Fl. 3
Ob. 1, 2
E. Hn.
Cl. 1, 2 in B♭
B. Cl. in B♭
Bn. 1, 2
Hn. 1, 2 in F
Hn. 3, 4 in F
Tpt. 1, 2 in B♭
Tpt. 3 in B♭
Trb. 1, 2
Trb. 3 Tb.
Timp.
Sn. Dr.
Cym. B. Dr.
Hp.
Vn. 1
Vn. 2
Va.
Vc.
Cb.
a 2
[a 2]
[1]
tr
mf
[mf]
[f]
p
mp
cresc.
[cresc.]
div.
[div.]
[unis.]

Florence Price

208
Picc.
tr
[f]
a 2
Fl. 1, 2
Fl. 3
[f]
Ob. 1, 2
E. Hn.
Cl. 1, 2 in B♭
B. Cl. in B♭
Bn. 1, 2
Hn. 1, 2 in F
Hn. 3, 4 in F
Tpt. 1, 2 in B♭
Tpt. 3 in B♭
Trb. 1, 2
Trb. 3 Tb.
Timp.
tr
Bells
f
Hp.
[l. v.]
mf
Vn. 1
Vn. 2
[div.]
Va.
Vc.
Cb.

Florence Price

218
accel.
Picc.
Fl. 1, 2
Fl. 3
Ob. 1, 2
E. Hn.
Cl. 1, 2 in B♭
B. Cl. in B♭
Bn. 1, 2
[a 2]
Hn. 1, 2 in F
Hn. 3, 4 in F
Tpt. 1, 2 in B♭
Tpt. 3 in B♭
Trb. 1, 2
Trb. 3 Tb.
a 2
Timp.
Sn. Dr.
Cym. B. Dr.
Cr. Cym.
Hp.
accel.
Vn. 1
Vn. 2
Va.
Vc.
[div.]
Cb.
cresc.
ff
[f]
[cresc.
[ff]

Florence Price

230
Tempo moderato
poco accel.
Andante
Picc.
Fl. 1, 2
Fl. 3
Ob. 1, 2
E. Hn.
Cl. 1, 2 in B♭
B. Cl. in B♭
Bn. 1, 2
Hn. 1, 2 in F
Hn. 3, 4 in F
Tpt. 1, 2 in B♭
Tpt. 3 in B♭
Trb. 1, 2
Trb. 3 Tb.
Timp.
Hp.
Vn. 1
Vn. 2
Va.
Vc.
Cb.
[a 2]
a 2
mf
f
[f]
[mf]
cresc.
[cresc.]
tr
[div.]
[unis.]

Florence Price

239
Picc.
Fl. 1, 2
Fl. 3
Ob. 1, 2
E. Hn.
Cl. 1, 2 in B♭
[ff]
B. Cl. in B♭
Bn. 1, 2
Tpt. 1, 2 in B♭
[a 2]
ff
Tpt. 3 in B♭
[ff]
Trb. 1, 2
[a 2]
ff
[a 2]
Trb. 3 Tb.
ff
Timp.
tr
B. Dr.
[ff]
Cr. Cym.
[ff]
Vn. 1
Vn. 2
Va.
[unis.]
ff
[div.]
Vc.
ff
[div.]
Cb.
ff
[non div.]

246
rit.
Picc.
Fl. 1, 2
[a 2]
Fl. 3
Ob. 1, 2
E. Hn.
Cl. 1, 2 in B♭
B. Cl. in B♭
Bn. 1, 2
Hn. 1, 2 in F
Hn. 3, 4 in F
Tpt. 1, 2 in B♭
Tpt. 3 in B♭
Trb. 1, 2
[a 2]
Trb. 3 Tb.
Timp.
Sn. Dr.
Cym. B. Dr.
rit.
Vn. 1
Vn. 2
[non div.]
Va.
[div.]
Vc.
[div.]
Cb.

I I

Andante ma non troppo
rit.
a tempo
Piccolo
Flute 1, 2
Flute 3
Oboe 1, 2
1 solo
mp espress.
a 2
[mp]
[p]
English Horn
p
[1]
Clarinet 1, 2 in B♭
p
Bass Clarinet in B♭
Bassoon 1, 2
p
Horn 1, 2 in F
Horn 3, 4 in F
Trumpet 1, 2 in B♭
Trumpet 3 in B♭
Trombone 1, 2
Trombone 3 Tuba
Timpani
Triangle
Celesta
Harp
Andante ma non troppo
rit.
a tempo
con sord.
Violin 1
mp
p
[con sord.]
Violin 2
[mp]
p
[div.]
con sord.
Viola
mp espress.
[p]
[div.]
con sord.
Violoncello
p
con sord.
Contrabass
p

8
[rit.]
a tempo
espress.
rit.
Picc.
mp cresc.
[mp] espress.
Fl. 1, 2
mp cresc.
mf
Fl. 3
[mp] [cresc.
] [mf]
a 2
Ob. 1, 2
Cl. 1, 2
in B♭
[1]
mp cresc.
1
mf
Tpt. 1, 2
in B♭
1
p
mf
mp
Hp.
p
[rit.]
a tempo
[remove mute]
rit.
Vn. 1
p
mf espress.
remove mute
Vn. 2
[p]
[mf] espress.
[remove mute]
Va.
p
mp espress.
[remove mute]
Vc.
p
[p]
[remove mute]
Cb.
p
p
16
a tempo
[1] solo
Cl. 1, 2
in B♭
mp
mf
a tempo
[div.]
[unis.]
Vn. 1
pp
f
p
mp
p
[div.]
[unis.]
Vn. 2
[pp]
[f]
[p]
[mp]
[p]
[unis.]
Va.
pp
f
p
mp
p
Vc.
pp
f
p
mp
p

23
Fl. 1, 2
Fl. 3
Ob. 1, 2
Bn. 1, 2
Cel.
Vn. 1
Vn. 2
Va.
Vc.
[div.]
[unis.]
[1]
29
rit.
a tempo
Picc.
Timp.
[1] solo
cre - - - scen- - - do
tr

Florence Price

48
poco rit.
a tempo
Fl. 1, 2
Fl. 3
Ob. 1, 2
E. Hn.
Cl. 1, 2 in B♭
B. Cl. in B♭
Bn. 1, 2
Tpt. 1 in B♭
Tpt. 2, 3 in B♭
Trb. 1, 2
Trb. 3 Tb.
Timp.
Vn. 1
Vn. 2
Va.
Vc.
Cb.
mf
f
[f]
[a 2]
a 2
solo
mp espress.
p
tr
[unis.]

poco rit.
solo
a tempo
rit.
Tpt. 1 in B♭
Tpt. 2, 3 in B♭
Trb. 1, 2
Trb. 3 Tb.
Trgl.
Hp.
[simile]
Vn. 1
Vn. 2
Va.
Vc.
[div.]
mf espress.
[unis.]
[non div.]
a tempo
Fl. 1, 2
Fl. 3
Tpt. 1, 2 in B♭
Tpt. 3 in B♭
Cel.
mf espress.

66
Picc.
Fl. 1, 2
Fl. 3
Cl. 1, 2 in B♭
Bn. 1, 2
Tpt. 1, 2 in B♭
Tpt. 3 in B♭
Trb. 1, 2
Trb. 3 Tb.
Cel.
Vn. 1
Vn. 2
Va.
Vc.
Cb.
pp
[a 2]
mf
[mf]
[div.]
con sord.
unis.
mp
[con sord.]
[mp]
[div.]
con sord.
mp
[unis.]
con sord.
mp
cresc.
[div.]
[cresc.]
cresc.
[cresc.]

71
Bn. 1, 2
Vn. 1
Vn. 2
Va.
Vc.
Cb.
poco accel.
poco rit.
a tempo
remove sord.
[remove sord.]
sur la touche
[sur la touche]
[unis.]
[div.]
76
Fl. 1, 2
Fl. 3
Ob. 1, 2
Cl. 1, 2 in B♭
Bn. 1, 2
Vn. 1
Vn. 2
Va.
Vc.
Cb.
a 2
poco rit.
[ord.]
[unis.]

80
a tempo
Picc.
Fl. 1, 2
Fl. 3
Ob. 1, 2
E. Hn.
Cl. 1, 2 in B♭
B. Cl. in B♭
Bn. 1, 2
Hn. 1, 2 in F
Hn. 3, 4 in F
Tpt. 1, 2 in B♭
Tpt. 3 in B♭
Trb. 1, 2
Trb. 3 Tb.
Timp.
Cel.
Hp.
a 2
a tempo
Vn. 1
Vn. 2
Va.
Vc.
Cb.
[div.]
[div.]

Florence Price

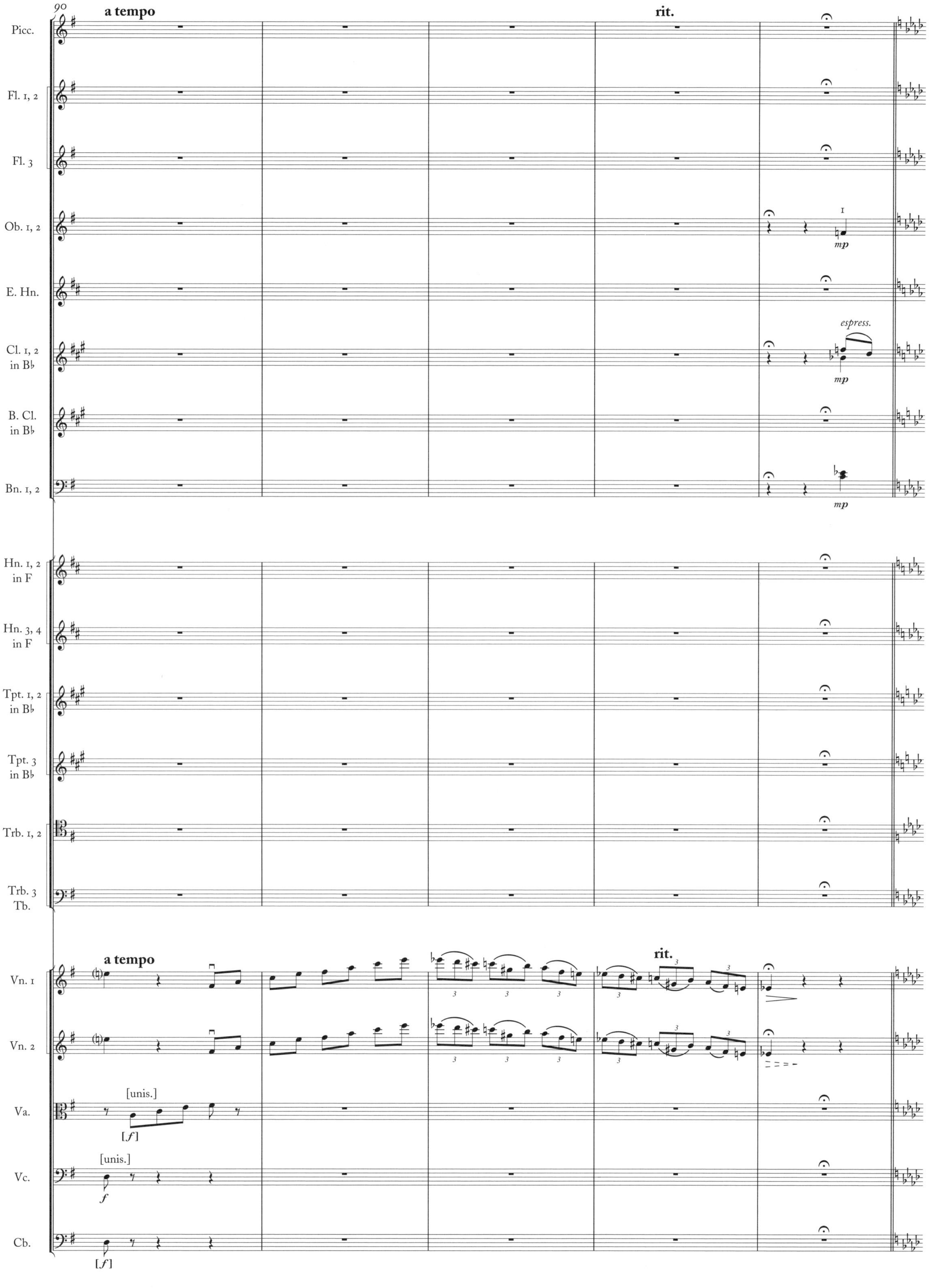
90
a tempo
rit.
Picc.
Fl. 1, 2
Fl. 3
Ob. 1, 2
E. Hn.
Cl. 1, 2 in B♭
B. Cl. in B♭
Bn. 1, 2
Hn. 1, 2 in F
Hn. 3, 4 in F
Tpt. 1, 2 in B♭
Tpt. 3 in B♭
Trb. 1, 2
Trb. 3 Tb.
Vn. 1
Vn. 2
Va.
Vc.
Cb.
espress.
mp
[unis.]
[f]
f

95
a tempo
poco rit.
a tempo
Picc.
Fl. 1, 2
Fl. 3
Ob. 1, 2
E. Hn.
Cl. 1, 2 in B♭
B. Cl. in B♭
Bn. 1, 2
Hn. 1, 2 in F
Hn. 3, 4 in F
Tpt. 1, 2 in B♭
Tpt. 3 in B♭
Trb. 1, 2
Trb. 3 Tb.
Timp.
Hp.
Vn. 1
Vn. 2
Va.
Vc.
Cb.
[a 2]
mf espress.
mp espress.
[mf][espress.]
[div.]
espress.

101
poco rit.
a tempo
espress.
Picc.
Fl. 1, 2
Fl. 3
Ob. 1, 2
E. Hn.
Cl. 1, 2 in B♭
B. Cl. in B♭
Bn. 1, 2
Hn. 1, 2 in F
Hn. 3, 4 in F
Tpt. 1, 2 in B♭
Tpt. 3 in B♭
Trb. 1, 2
Trb. 3 Tb.
Timp.
Hp.
Vn. 1
Vn. 2
Va.
Vc.
Cb.
mp
cresc.
[1]
[div.]

Florence Price

118
poco rit.
Fl. 1, 2
Fl. 3
Ob. 1, 2
E. Hn.
Cl. 1, 2 in B♭
B. Cl. in B♭
Bn. 1, 2
Hn. 1, 2 in F
Hn. 3, 4 in F
Tpt. 1, 2 in B♭
Tpt. 3 in B♭
Cel.
Vn. 1
Vn. 2
Va.
Vc.
Cb.
mp cresc.
espress.
[1]
[div.]
[unis.]
poco rit.

125
a tempo
rit.
a tempo
Fl. 1, 2
Fl. 3
Ob. 1, 2
E. Hn.
Cl. 1, 2 in B♭
B. Cl. in B♭
Bn. 1, 2
Hn. 1, 2 in F
Hn. 3, 4 in F
Tpt. 1, 2 in B♭
Tpt. 3 in B♭
Cel.
Vn. 1
Vn. 2
Va.
Vc.
Cb.
[1]
[a 2]
mf
mp cresc. molto
1 dolce
p
cresc.
espress.
mp
[mp]
[mp] [cresc. molto
[div.]
[unis.]

a tempo
[a 2]
133
rit.
Fl. 1, 2
Fl. 3
Ob. 1, 2
E. Hn.
Cl. 1, 2 in B♭
B. Cl. in B♭
Bn. 1, 2
Hn. 1, 2 in F
Hn. 3, 4 in F
Tpt. 1, 2 in B♭
Tpt. 3 in B♭
Trb. 1, 2
Trb. 3 Tb.
Bells
Hp.
Vn. 1
Vn. 2
Va.
Vc.
Cb.
cresc. molto
[poco meno forte]

III. JUBA

Florence Price

6
Picc.
Fl. 1, 2
[a 2]
Fl. 3
Ob. 1, 2
E. Hn.
Cl. 1, 2 in B♭
[a 2]
B. Cl. in B♭
Bn. 1, 2
[a 2]
Hn. 1, 2 in F
Hn. 3, 4 in F
Tpt. 1, 2 in B♭
Tpt. 3 in B♭
Trb. 1, 2
Trb. 3 Tb.
Timp.
Sn. Dr.
Cym. B. Dr.
Vn. 1
Vn. 2
Va.
[div.]
[unis.]
Vc.
[div.]
[unis.]
Cb.

Florence Price

20
[a 2]
Fl. 1, 2
Fl. 3
Ob. 1, 2
E. Hn.
Cl. 1, 2 in B♭
B. Cl. in B♭
Bn. 1, 2
Hn. 1, 2 in F
Hn. 3, 4 in F
Tpt. 1, 2 in B♭
Tpt. 3 in B♭
Trb. 1, 2
Trb. 3 Tb.
Timp.
Sn. Dr.
Cym. B. Dr.
Sd. Pa. Cast.
Bells
Vn. 1
Vn. 2
Va.
Vc.
Cb.
[div.]
[unis.]
[arco]

27
Picc.
Fl. 1, 2
Fl. 3
Ob. 1, 2
E. Hn.
Cl. 1, 2 in B♭
B. Cl. in B♭
Bn. 1, 2
Hn. 1, 2 in F
Hn. 3, 4 in F
Tpt. 1, 2 in B♭
Tpt. 3 in B♭
Trb. 1, 2
Trb. 3 Tb.
Timp.
Sn. Dr.
Cym. B. Dr.
Cr. Cym.
Vn. 1
Vn. 2
Va.
Vc.
Cb.
[a 2]
cresc.
[f] [non legato]
f non legato
[dim.]
dim.
plate roll
[unis.]
[div.]
[cresc.]
[1]

33
Picc.
Fl. 1, 2
Fl. 3
Ob. 1, 2
E. Hn.
Cl. 1, 2 in B♭
B. Cl. in B♭
Bn. 1, 2
Hn. 1, 2 in F
Hn. 3, 4 in F
Tpt. 1, 2 in B♭
Tpt. 3 in B♭
Trb. 1, 2
Trb. 3 Tb.
Timp.
Sn. Dr.
Cym. B. Dr.
Cr. Cym.
Vn. 1
Vn. 2
Va.
Vc.
Cb.
[div.]
[unis.]
tr

Florence Price

45
Picc.
Fl. 1, 2
Fl. 3
Ob. 1, 2
E. Hn.
Cl. 1, 2 in B♭
B. Cl. in B♭
Bn. 1, 2
Hn. 1, 2 in F
Hn. 3, 4 in F
Tpt. 1, 2 in B♭
Tpt. 3 in B♭
Trb. 1, 2
Trb. 3 Tb.
Timp.
Sn. Dr.
B. Dr.
Vn. 1
Vn. 2
Va.
Vc.
Cb.
[a 2]
a 2
[div.]
[unis.]
div.
p
mp
[mp]

Florence Price

57
Picc.
Fl. 1, 2
Fl. 3
Ob. 1, 2
E. Hn.
Cl. 1, 2 in B♭
B. Cl. in B♭
Bn. 1, 2
Hn. 1, 2 in F
Hn. 3, 4 in F
Tpt. 1, 2 in B♭
Tpt. 3 in B♭
Trb. 1, 2
Trb. 3 Tb.
Timp.
Sn. Dr.
Cym. B. Dr.
Trgl.
Sd. Pa. Cast.
Vn. 1
Vn. 2
Va.
Vc.
Cb.
tr
mf
[a 2]
[mf]
[regular sticks]
[unis.]
div.
[mp]

Florence Price

69
Picc.
Fl. 1, 2
Fl. 3
Ob. 1, 2
E. Hn.
Cl. 1, 2 in B♭
B. Cl. in B♭
Bn. 1, 2
Hn. 1, 2 in F
Hn. 3, 4 in F
Tpt. 1, 2 in B♭
Tpt. 3 in B♭
Trb. 1, 2
Trb. 3 Tb.
Timp.
Sn. Dr.
Cym. B. Dr.
Trgl.
Wd. Bl.
Sd. Pa. Cast.
Vn. 1
Vn. 2
Va.
Vc.
Cb.
tr
[a 2]
[mp]
wire brush
[mf]
p
[div.]
[unis.]
div.

Florence Price

81
Picc.
Fl. 1, 2
Fl. 3
Ob. 1, 2
E. Hn.
Cl. 1, 2 in B♭
B. Cl. in B♭
Bn. 1, 2
Hn. 1, 2 in F
Hn. 3, 4 in F
Tpt. 1, 2 in B♭
Tpt. 3 in B♭
Trb. 1, 2
Trb. 3 Tb.
Timp.
Sn. Dr.
Cym. B. Dr.
Sd. Pa. Cast.
Vn. 1
Vn. 2
Va.
Vc.
Cb.
[a 2]
mf
[mf]
div.
[div.]
[unis.]
arco

Florence Price

93
Andantino
Ob. 1, 2
E. Hn.
Cl. 1, 2 in B♭
Bn. 1, 2
tin mutes
mp
Tpt. 1, 2 in B♭
mf
[tin mute]
Tpt. 3 in B♭
[mp]
mf
[mutes on]
2
Trb. 1, 2
mf
Trb. 3 Tb.
Sn. Dr.
B. Dr.
p
mp
Wd. Bl.
mp
mf
Sd. Pa.
Andantino
Vn. 1
Vn. 2
pizz.
Va.
mf
[mp]
mf
[unis.]
pizz.
Vc.
mf
[mp]
mf
pizz.
Cb.
mf
[mp]
mf

Florence Price

105
[a 2]
Fl. 1, 2
Fl. 3
Ob. 1, 2
E. Hn.
Cl. 1, 2 in B♭
B. Cl. in B♭
Bn. 1, 2
Tpt. 1, 2 in B♭
Tpt. 3 in B♭
Trb. 1, 2
Trb. 3 Tb.
B. Dr.
Wd. Bl.
Vn. 1
Vn. 2
Va.
Vc.
Cb.
pizz.
pizz.

poco rit.
rit.
[Tempo primo]
Fl. 1, 2
E. Hn.
mf espress.
Cl. 1, 2 in B♭
mf [espress.]
in A
Bn. 1, 2
Tpt. 1, 2 in B♭
Tpt. 3 in B♭
Trb. 1, 2
Trb. 3 Tb.
Sn. Dr.
Cym. B. Dr.
Trgl.
Vn. 1
Vn. 2
Va.
arco
div.
[unis.]
Vc.
Cb.
[arco]

117
Fl. 1, 2
Fl. 3
E. Hn.
Cl. 1, 2 in A
[a 2]
B. Cl. in B♭
Bn. 1, 2
Hn. 1, 2 in F
Hn. 3, 4 in F
Tpt. 1, 2 in A
Tpt. 3 in A
Trb. 1, 2
Trb. 3 Tb.
Sn. Dr.
Cym. B. Dr.
Trgl.
tr
Vn. 1
p subito
Vn. 2
[p] [subito]
div.
Va.
Vc.
Cb.

Florence Price

131
Picc.
Fl. 1, 2
Fl. 3
Ob. 1, 2
E. Hn.
Cl. 1, 2 in A
B. Cl. in B♭
Bn. 1, 2
Hn. 1, 2 in F
Hn. 3, 4 in F
Tpt. 1, 2 in A
Tpt. 3 in A
Trb. 1, 2
Trb. 3 Tb.
Sn. Dr.
Cym. B. Dr.
Trgl.
Cast.
Vn. 1
Vn. 2
Va.
Vc.
Cb.
[a 2]
[unis.]
p subito
[p] [subito]
pp subito
div.

Florence Price

144
rit.
Picc.
Fl. 1, 2
[a 2]
Fl. 3
Ob. 1, 2
E. Hn.
Cl. 1, 2 in A
in B♭
B. Cl. in B♭
Bn. 1, 2
a 2
Hn. 1, 2 in F
Hn. 3, 4 in F
Tpt. 1, 2 in A
in B♭
Tpt. 3 in A
in B♭
Trb. 1, 2
Trb. 3 Tb.
a 2
Sn. Dr.
Cym. B. Dr.
Cast.
rit.
Vn. 1
Vn. 2
Va.
[unis.]
div.
Vc.
Cb.

Andantino
[1] solo [through m. 157 only if no xylophone]
151
Fl. 1, 2
Fl. 3
Ob. 1, 2
Cl. 1, 2 in B♭
Hn. 1, 2 in F
Hn. 3, 4 in F
Tpt. 1, 2 in B♭
Tpt. 3 in B♭
Trb. 1, 2
Trb. 3 Tb.
Wd. Bl.
Xyl.
solo
[ad lib: tremolo throughout]
Andantino
Vn. 1
Vn. 2
Va.
Vc.
Cb.
[div.]
[unis.]
pizz.

più mosso - - - - accel.
158
Fl. 1, 2
p
[a 2]
mf cresc.
Fl. 3
[mf] [cresc.
Ob. 1, 2
[a 2]
mf
Cl. 1, 2 in B♭
[play only if no xylophone through m. 162]
[a 2]
cre - - - - - scen - - - - - do
Hn. 1, 2 in F
Hn. 3, 4 in F
[mp]
Tpt. 1, 2 in B♭
Tpt. 3 in B♭
Trb. 1, 2
Trb. 3 Tb.
Wd. Bl.
Xyl.
cre - - - - - scen - - - - - do
più mosso - - - - accel.
Vn. 1
cre - - - - - scen - - - - - do
Vn. 2
[cre - - - - - scen - - - - - do - - - - -]
Va.
div.
[unis.]
[arco]
mf cresc.
Vc.
div.
div.
[arco]
f
Cb.
[arco]
f

Tempo primo

Florence Price

171
Picc.
Fl. 1, 2
Fl. 3
Ob. 1, 2
E. Hn.
Cl. 1, 2 in B♭
B. Cl. in B♭
Bn. 1, 2
Hn. 1, 2 in F
Hn. 3, 4 in F
Tpt. 1, 2 in B♭
Tpt. 3 in B♭
Trb. 1, 2
Trb. 3 Tb.
Timp.
Sn. Dr.
Cym. B. Dr.
Slap.
Xyl.
Vn. 1
Vn. 2
Va.
Vc.
Cb.
[a 2]
[unis.]
[div.]
div.
[2]

177
Picc.
Fl. 1, 2
Fl. 3
Ob. 1, 2
E. Hn.
Cl. 1, 2 in B♭
B. Cl. in B♭
Bn. 1, 2
Hn. 1, 2 in F
Hn. 3, 4 in F
Tpt. 1, 2 in B♭
Tpt. 3 in B♭
Trb. 1, 2
Trb. 3 Tb.
Timp.
Sn. Dr.
Cym. B. Dr.
Vn. 1
Vn. 2
Va.
Vc.
Cb.
[a 2]
[1]
tr
div.
mf
[mf]
cre
mf cre

183
Picc.
Fl. 1, 2
Fl. 3
Ob. 1, 2
E. Hn.
Cl. 1, 2 in B♭
B. Cl. in B♭
Bn. 1, 2
Hn. 1, 2 in F
Hn. 3, 4 in F
Tpt. 1, 2 in B♭
Tpt. 3 in B♭
Trb. 1, 2
Trb. 3 Tb.
Timp.
Sn. Dr.
Cym. B. Dr.
Vn. 1
Vn. 2
Va.
Vc.
Cb.
f cresc.
scen
do
ff
[ff]
[a 2]
[f]
f
tr
div.
[div.]

Florence Price

IV. SCHERZO. FINALE

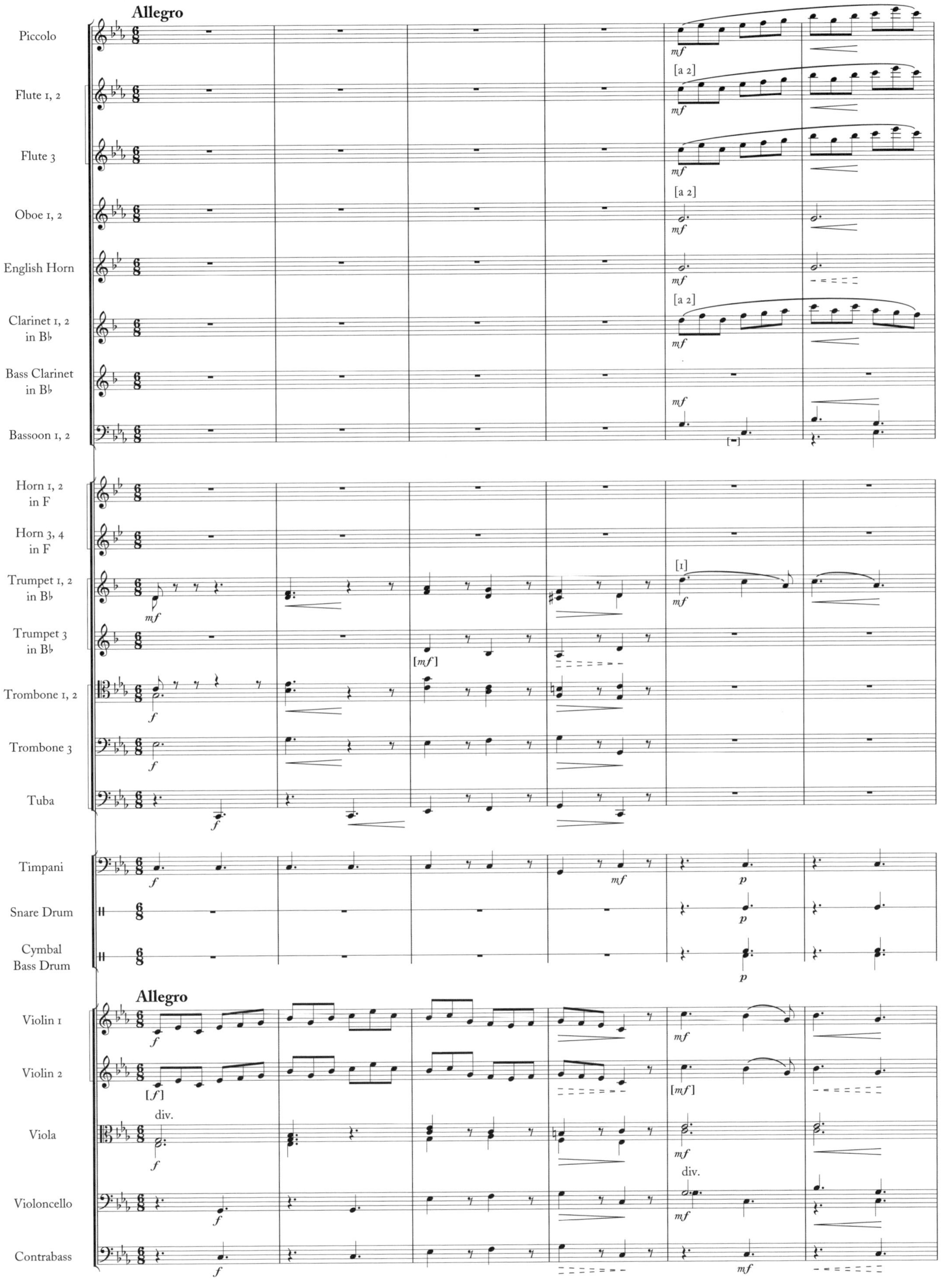

Florence Price

13
Picc.
Fl. 1, 2
Fl. 3
Ob. 1, 2
E. Hn.
Cl. 1, 2 in B♭
B. Cl. in B♭
Bn. 1, 2
Hn. 1, 2 in F
Hn. 3, 4 in F
Tpt. 1, 2 in B♭
Tpt. 3 in B♭
Trb. 1, 2
Trb. 3 Tb.
Timp.
Sn. Dr.
Cym. B. Dr.
Vn. 1
Vn. 2
Va.
Vc.
Cb.
[a 2]
[unis.]
[mf] cresc.
mf
cresc.
f
p
pp
mp
[mp]
tr

19
Picc.
Fl. 1, 2
Fl. 3
Ob. 1, 2
E. Hn.
Cl. 1, 2 in B♭
B. Cl. in B♭
Bn. 1, 2
Hn. 1, 2 in F
Hn. 3, 4 in F
Tpt. 1, 2 in B♭
Tpt. 3 in B♭
Trb. 1, 2
Trb. 3 Tb.
Timp.
Sn. Dr.
Cym. B. Dr.
Vn. 1
Vn. 2
Va.
Vc.
Cb.
[a 2]
[1]
solo
div.
[unis.]
mf
mp
p
cre- - - - - - scen- - - - do- - - -
[mf] [cresc.]
tr

26
Picc.
Fl. 1, 2
[a 2]
Fl. 3
Ob. 1, 2
E. Hn.
Cl. 1, 2 in B♭
[a 2]
B. Cl. in B♭
Bn. 1, 2
Hn. 1, 2 in F
Hn. 3, 4 in F
[a 2]
Tpt. 1, 2 in B♭
Tpt. 3 in B♭
Trb. 1, 2
Trb. 3 Tb.
Timp.
Sn. Dr.
Cym. B. Dr.
Cr. Cym.
Vn. 1
Vn. 2
Va.
[unis.]
div.
Vc.
[unis.]
div.
Cb.

Florence Price

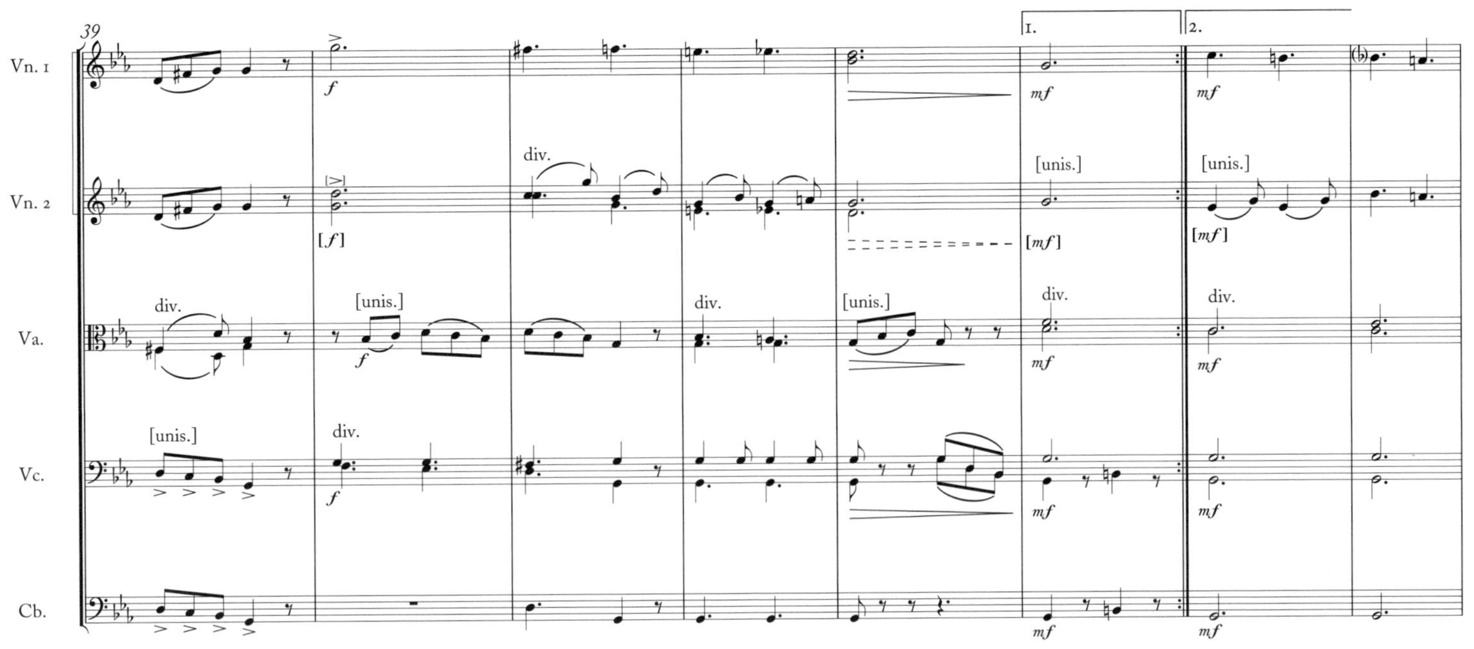
39
Vn. 1
Vn. 2
Va.
Vc.
Cb.
1.
2.
div.
[unis.]
f
[f]
mf
[mf]

46
Cl. 1, 2 in B♭
Bn. 1, 2
Hn. 1, 2 in F
Hn. 3, 4 in F
Vn. 1
Vn. 2
Va.
Vc.
Cb.
[1]
[unis.]
mf
[mf]
pp
[pp]

Florence Price

59
Picc.
Fl. 1, 2
Fl. 3
Ob. 1, 2
E. Hn.
Cl. 1, 2 in B♭
B. Cl. in B♭
Bn. 1, 2
Tpt. 1, 2 in B♭
Tpt. 3 in B♭
Trb. 1, 2
Trb. 3 Tb.
Timp.
Sn. Dr.
Cym. B. Dr.
Trgl. Cr. Cym.
Cast.
Vn. 1
Vn. 2
Va.
Vc.
Cb.
[a 2]
[1]
[unis.]
[div.]
cresc.

Florence Price

71
Fl. 1, 2
Fl. 3
Ob. 1, 2
E. Hn.
Cl. 1, 2 in B♭
Bn. 1, 2
Hn. 1, 2 in F
Hn. 3, 4 in F
Tpt. 1, 2 in B♭
Tpt. 3 in B♭
Trb. 1, 2
Trb. 3 Tb.
Vn. 1
Vn. 2
Va.
Vc.
Cb.
[a 2]
a 2
mf
1
div.
[unis.]
[mf]

Florence Price

83
Picc.
Fl. 1, 2
Fl. 3
Ob. 1, 2
E. Hn.
Cl. 1, 2 in B♭
B. Cl. in B♭
[a 2]
Bn. 1, 2
mp
Hn. 1, 2 in F
Hn. 3, 4 in F
Tpt. 1, 2 in B♭
Tpt. 3 in B♭
Trb. 1, 2
Trb. 3 Tb.
Timp.
Sn. Dr.
Cym. B. Dr.
Vn. 1
Vn. 2
Va.
Vc.
[unis.]
[div.]
[unis.]
mp
Cb.
mp

89
rit.
a tempo
Picc.
Fl. 1, 2
Fl. 3
Ob. 1, 2
E. Hn.
Cl. 1, 2 in B♭
B. Cl. in B♭
[a 2]
Bn. 1, 2
cre- scen- do
Hn. 1, 2 in F
Hn. 3, 4 in F
Tpt. 1, 2 in B♭
Tpt. 3 in B♭
Trb. 1, 2
Trb. 3 Tb.
Timp.
Sn. Dr.
Cym. B. Dr.
rit.
a tempo
Vn. 1
Vn. 2
Va.
mp cre- scen- do
Vc.
Cb.
[cre-] scen do

95
Picc.
Fl. 1, 2
Fl. 3
Ob. 1, 2
E. Hn.
Cl. 1, 2 in B♭
B. Cl. in B♭
Bn. 1, 2
Hn. 1, 2 in F
Hn. 3, 4 in F
Tpt. 1, 2 in B♭
Tpt. 3 in B♭
Trb. 1, 2
Trb. 3 Tb.
Timp.
Sn. Dr.
Cym. B. Dr.
Vn. 1
Vn. 2
Va.
Vc.
Cb.
[a 2]
espress.
[espress.]
sf
tr

Florence Price

108
Picc.
Fl. 1, 2
Fl. 3
Ob. 1, 2
E. Hn.
Cl. 1, 2 in B♭
B. Cl. in B♭
Bn. 1, 2
Hn. 1, 2 in F
Hn. 3, 4 in F
Tpt. 1, 2 in B♭
Tpt. 3 in B♭
Trb. 1, 2
Trb. 3 Tb.
Timp.
Sn. Dr.
Cym. B. Dr.
Vn. 1
Vn. 2
Va.
Vc.
Cb.
[a 2]
[non div.]

Florence Price

SYMPHONY NO. 3 IN C MINOR, MOVEMENT IV

127
Picc.
Fl. 1, 2
Fl. 3
Ob. 1, 2
E. Hn.
Cl. 1, 2 in B♭
B. Cl. in B♭
Bn. 1, 2
Hn. 1, 2 in F
Hn. 3, 4 in F
Tpt. 1, 2 in B♭
Tpt. 3 in B♭
Trb. 1, 2
Trb. 3 Tb.
Timp.
Sn. Dr.
Cym. B. Dr.
Cr. Cym.
Vn. 1
Vn. 2
Va.
Vc.
Cb.
[a 2]
tr
[non div.]

134
Picc.
Fl. 1, 2
Fl. 3
Ob. 1, 2
E. Hn.
Cl. 1, 2 in B♭
[a 2]
Tpt. 1, 2 in B♭
Tpt. 3 in B♭
Trb. 1, 2
[a 2]
Trb. 3 Tb.
Timp.
Sn. Dr.
Cym. B. Dr.
Vn. 1
8va
mf
Vn. 2
[mf]
Va.
[div.]
[unis.]
mf
Vc.
[unis.]
mf
Cb.

Florence Price

155
Picc.
[mf] [cre - scen - do
f
Fl. 1, 2
[scen - do
f
Fl. 3
[scen - do
f
Ob. 1, 2
[scen - do
f
E. Hn.
Cl. 1, 2 in B♭
[scen - do
f
B. Cl. in B♭
Bn. 1, 2
[scen - do
f
f
[mp] cresc. molto
Hn. 1, 2 in F
[scen - do
f
Hn. 3, 4 in F
scen - do -]
[f]
Tpt. 1, 2 in B♭
Tpt. 3 in B♭
Trb. 1, 2
[a 2]
f
mp
Trb. 3
f
mp
Tb.
[f]
mp
Timp.
f
Sn. Dr.
Cym. B. Dr.
plate roll
tr
Cr. Cym.
[mp]
Gong
Vn. 1
f cresc. molto
Vn. 2
[f] [cresc. molto]
Va.
f cresc. molto
Vc.
mf
[cresc.
[f]
f
[cresc. molto]
Cb.
mf
[cresc.
[f]
[f]
[cresc. molto]

Florence Price

169
meno mosso
rit.
Picc.
Fl. 1, 2
[a 2]
Fl. 3
Ob. 1, 2
E. Hn.
[ff]
Cl. 1, 2 in B♭
[a 2]
1
mp
B. Cl. in B♭
Bn. 1, 2
[a 2]
Hn. 1, 2 in F
Hn. 3, 4 in F
Tpt. 1, 2 in B♭
Tpt. 3 in B♭
Trb. 1, 2
[a 2]
Trb. 3 Tb.
Timp.
meno mosso
rit.
Vn. 1
Vn. 2
Va.
[div.]
Vc.
[unis.]
Cb.

176
a tempo [= meno mosso]
[rit.]
a tempo [= Tempo primo]
Picc.
Fl. 1, 2
Fl. 3
Ob. 1, 2
E. Hn.
Cl. 1, 2 in B♭
B. Cl. in B♭
Bn. 1, 2
[a 2]
Hn. 1, 2 in F
Hn. 3, 4 in F
Tpt. 1, 2 in B♭
Tpt. 3 in B♭
Trb. 1, 2
Trb. 3 Tb.
Timp.
Vn. 1
Vn. 2
Va.
div.
Vc.
Cb.
cresc.

184
Picc.
Fl. 1, 2
Fl. 3
Ob. 1, 2
E. Hn.
Cl. 1, 2 in B♭
B. Cl. in B♭
Bn. 1, 2
Hn. 1, 2 in F
Hn. 3, 4 in F
Tpt. 1, 2 in B♭
Tpt. 3 in B♭
Trb. 1, 2
Trb. 3 Tb.
Timp.
Sn. Dr.
Cym. B. Dr.
Vn. 1
Vn. 2
Va.
Vc.
Cb.
[a 2]
[mp] cresc.
unis.
[div.]
[unis.]

Florence Price

196
Picc.
Fl. 1, 2
Fl. 3
Ob. 1, 2
E. Hn.
Cl. 1, 2 in B♭
B. Cl. in B♭
Bn. 1, 2
Hn. 1, 2 in F
Hn. 3, 4 in F
Tpt. 1, 2 in B♭
Tpt. 3 in B♭
Trb. 1, 2
Trb. 3 Tb.
Timp.
Sn. Dr.
Cym. B. Dr.
Vn. 1
Vn. 2
Va.
Vc.
Cb.
sf
[sf]
div.
[div.]

Florence Price

209
rit.
a tempo
Picc.
Fl. 1, 2
[a 2]
Fl. 3
Ob. 1, 2
E. Hn.
Cl. 1, 2 in B♭
B. Cl. in B♭
Bn. 1, 2
Hn. 1, 2 in F
Hn. 3, 4 in F
Tpt. 1, 2 in B♭
Tpt. 3 in B♭
Trb. 1, 2
Trb. 3 Tb.
Timp.
Tamb. Sn. Dr.
Cym. B. Dr.
Cr. Cym.
Vn. 1
Vn. 2
Va.
[unis.]
Vc.
pizz.
arco
Cb.
[arco]

Florence Price

223
Picc.
Fl. 1, 2
Fl. 3
Ob. 1, 2
E. Hn.
Cl. 1, 2 in B♭
B. Cl. in B♭
Bn. 1, 2
Hn. 1, 2 in F
Hn. 3, 4 in F
Tpt. 1, 2 in B♭
Tpt. 3 in B♭
Trb. 1, 2
Trb. 3 Tb.
Timp.
Tamb. Sn. Dr.
Cym. B. Dr.
Trgl. Cr. Cym.
Gong
Vn. 1
Vn. 2
Va.
Vc.
Cb.
div.
[unis.]
8va
cresc.
ff
fff
tr

Florence Price

237
Andante
rit.
a tempo
Picc.
Fl. 1, 2
Fl. 3
Ob. 1, 2
E. Hn.
Cl. 1, 2 in B♭
B. Cl. in B♭
Bn. 1, 2
Hn. 1, 2 in F
Hn. 3, 4 in F
Tpt. 1, 2 in B♭
Tpt. 3 in B♭
Trb. 1, 2
Trb. 3 Tb.
Timp.
Sn. Dr.
B. Dr.
2 Cym.
Vn. 1
Vn. 2
Va.
Vc.
Cb.
[a 2]
[non div.]
[unis.]
plate roll
[plate roll]
pizz.
ff
ffz
[ff]
[ffz]

APPARATUS

Wayne Shirley

Sources

Primary Sources

The Symphony no. 1 in E Minor has a single extant source with authority, the electropositive photocopy of the composer's holograph manuscript now in the Florence Price Collection in the David W. Mullins Library of the University of Arkansas, Fayetteville, Arkansas. The current whereabouts of the manuscript itself are not known. The photocopy was made by the composer's daughter, Florence Price Robinson, for Mary Dengler Hudgins in 1968 to aid in Hudgins's research into the music of Arkansas composers, and was given by Robinson to the University of Arkansas. Except in cases where we must take the nature of the photocopy into consideration, we shall discuss the score of the first symphony in terms of the lost original, since this will make for a less confusing editorial report.

The main source of the Symphony no. 3 in C minor is the holograph manuscript full score presented by the composer to Carl Van Vechten, now in the James Weldon Johnson Collection in the Beinecke Rare Book Library of Yale University, the gift of Carl Van Vechten.[1] This is not the only source with authority for the third symphony. There are also photocopies of three pages of parts, in the composer's hand, in the Florence Price Collection at the University of Arkansas. These photocopies—single pages, faded and difficult to read—change no readings in MUSA's edition, but they have been helpful in editing.

Both of the full scores are in the composer's ink hand, which changes relatively little from 1932 to 1939. Both are on Carl Fischer Monarch Brand no. 22 paper—a general-use 24-staff paper without instrumental designations. Otherwise the scores are considerably different.

The score of the third symphony (**3A**) is in standard concert-score format, with each page presenting the entire orchestra, including instruments silent on that page, in the standard configuration. The strings, despite Price's idiosyncratic method of scoring, which will be discussed below, are in the standard format, with Violin 1 and 2 given separate staves and Viola, Cello, and Bass given one staff each. Price has numbered the first and last measures of each page from the start of the symphony through m. 107 of the third movement and from m. 166 of the fourth movement to the end (thus not

---

1. "The James Weldon Johnson Collection" is the name assigned to all of Carl Van Vechten's gifts of African-American materials to Yale University. The fact that the third symphony is in this collection does not imply a connection between Price and James Weldon Johnson.

numbering mm. 131–47 of the third movement, where we contend that a measure has been repeated). There are a few changes made in red pencil, occurring in mm. 169–72 and 192–95 of the fourth movement. Although a few instrumental names have been written in red ink at important entrances, there are no conductor's marks in the score whatsoever; it is clear that the score has not been used for performance. It is possible to explain the lack of conductor's marks by suggesting that a photostat of this score was used for performance; it is more likely, however, that this score represents a fresh writing out of the piece as a gift to Van Vechten and that the original score is lost. At least one spot in the three surviving pages of parts strongly suggests the existence of an earlier score.

Three single pages of parts for the third symphony exist in the Florence Price Collection at the University of Arkansas (**3B**). All three pages are in Price's hand, in ink. They are, in progressive order of significance:

1. Violin 1, stand 4, third movement (Juba), mm. 1–68: This part establishes that m. 53 in the first violins (and so, by extension, in the seconds) was a double-stop rather than a divisi in the first version of the symphony. The editors, thinking that the divisi will sound better, fall back on the ambiguity of **3A**. It is also the part that has most clearly been used in performance, containing several performer's markings (including "spiccato sempre" at the beginning). Otherwise the part is straightforward, differing from **3A** in some details of articulation (and making a copying mistake in mm. 62–63, slipping down to the Violin 2 part for two measures) but not challenging any of the readings of **3A**.

2. Horn 1, first movement, mm. 1–190: This part is most useful for confirming that the entry of Horns 1 and 2 in m. 32—a high entry unlike anything else in Price's horn writing—is indeed what the composer intended. It also misses a few of the tempo changes in **3A**; these may, however, be omissions in the copying of the part rather than indications that the part comes from another source.

3. Viola 2, first movement, mm. 114–96: This is the hardest of the three parts to read in its photocopied form, but the most significant in what it contains. The significance of its being a Viola 2 part (rather than a general Viola part) will be discussed below. Here we note that in this part mm. 194–96 are radically different from the Viola 2 part in **3A**. In **3A** (and in the MUSA edition), the violas straightforwardly double cellos and bassoons on the melody; in **3B**, Viola 2 plays fingered tremolo sixteenth-notes as part of the harmonic background. This is not a change that could comfortably have been made in copying; it argues strongly for a score of the third symphony either previous to or later than **3A**. The change—from complex to straightforward, from chancy to surefire—suggests that **3A** is the revised version.

The score of the first symphony **1A**) has also quite clearly not been used for performance. Otherwise it presents a quite different appearance from the score of the third symphony. Price seems to have modeled her score of the first symphony, her first considerable orchestral work, on the format of the study-score, with only the instruments that play on a particular system appearing on that system. Thus, there are often two separate systems on a single page. This leads to spots where instruments Price had not initially thought of using in that particular set of measures must be shoehorned into the score, often far from the spot where one would normally look for them. This presents occasional problems for the editors. By the fourth movement Price has abandoned this format for one in which each instrument gets its own line—including separate lines for Flutes 1 and 2, Oboes 1 and 2, Clarinets 1 and 2, Violas 1 and 2, and Cellos 1 and 2.

Three other features of the score of the first symphony will be clear from Plate 1, which shows the opening of the piece. One is the number of erasures in the manuscript—erasures presumably done with penknife. This is perhaps an inevitable consequence of a composer approaching her first major task of orchestration in ink, using a format as unforgiving as that of the study-score. The other two special features probably represent an attempt to make the work easier for the Wanamaker Prize committee. Accompanying much (though not all) of the score is a somewhat sketchy reduction, for solo piano ("for reader's convenience only" is written on the first page). In addition, the principal formal devices and sections in the first movement are labeled ("Basic motive" and "Prin[cipal] Theme" in Plate 1). There is also one such label in the fourth movement—"Theme reversed" at m. 242—labeling a retrograde of the main theme. The precise nature of a text involving erasure of ink manuscript by penknife can be difficult to decipher in a photocopy, as can the presence or absence of prolongation dots and staccato marks. We do not believe that any serious changes in the MUSA edition would be made if the original manuscript were discovered, but it would certainly help to clear up single measures in single instruments where it is difficult to tell which of two slightly differing readings is the final one.

Secondary Sources

No parts contemporary with Florence Price, save for the three single pages which make up **3B**, exist for either of the symphonies, nor do any sketches, nor any scores, complete or fragmentary, beyond **1A** and **3A**. There are, however, several scores and sets of parts written out in the years after Price's death. They have no authority independent of **1A** and **3A**; but all of them have been used for performance, and all save one have served as preparation for the present edition. They are as follows:

1B: A set of parts for the first symphony, extracted by an unknown copyist, in the Florence Price Collection at the University of Arkansas. This set of parts was prepared from **1A** for a performance by the North Arkansas Symphony Orchestra, probably in the 1970s. The parts bear the marks of being used in performance and are still available on loan for a fee from the University of Arkansas Library. No freshly prepared score created to go with these parts exists. This source was not used in the preparation of MUSA's edition.

1C: A score of the first symphony was generated in 1997 by entering the text of **1A** into a computer. This score is in standard format save that each wind instrument has its own line. This score and a set of parts generated from it has been used for several performances. It has no authority independent of **1A** but was important to the MUSA edition as a place to try out the problems of editing Price.

3C: In April–June 1998 a set of parts for the third symphony was prepared from a photocopy of **3A** by Wayne D. Shirley and Kevin LaVine for a performance on 25 June 1998 at the William Grant Still Festival at Flagstaff, Arizona.

3D: In August 1998 a score of the third symphony was created on a computer by Allen Menton. The score is, in general, based on **3A**, with corrections from **3C**. Since there was considerable demand for a performing edition, some minor adjustments—particularly the redistribution of double-stops in the strings— were made. Parts generated from this score have been used in several performances, including the performance by The Women's Philharmonic released as Koch International Classics 3-7518-2. Sources **3C** and **3D** have no authority independent of **3A**, but have been a useful early drafts for the MUSA edition; in particular they have brought to our attention spots where the notation, unedited, proves puzzling to performers.

EDITORIAL METHODS

Both symphonies are published here in the format that is standard for nineteenth- and twentieth-century scores of orchestral music: the standard order of instruments, two like instruments on a single line (three instruments—the three flutes and trumpets of the third symphony, the three trombones of each symphony—are printed two-and-one). For the third symphony this essentially reproduces the format of **3A**. For the first symphony, in which there are identical parts for identical instruments on two different lines, this involves putting on a single line what is on two lines in the manuscript. Dynamic markings appear below the instrumental lines to which they apply (unless, as happens very rarely in Price, two instruments on a single line have different dynamics); expression marks (e.g., "espress.," "marcato") appear above unless they are joined to a dynamic marking (e.g., "ƒ espress.").

EDITORIAL CHANGES

In general, editorial changes have been indicated either in brackets (ties and slurs appear dashed) or in the Apparatus. Some changes have been seen as so non-obtrusive as not to require documentation. These are:

1. Moving tempo directions to the top of the score and above the strings. Price occasionally indicates "accel" and "ritard" above the instruments that are most active.
2. Regularizing fermatas.
3. Particularly in the third symphony, Price often leaves off triplet-, quintolet-, or septolet-brackets. When the notation for these spots is completely clear, the addition of such brackets has not been noted. When another interpretation is possible, the addition of the triplet bracket is noted.

PRICE AND PHRASING

In general, Price phrases an individual line identically within a single family of instruments (woodwind, brass, strings). When such phrasings differ, the editors have usually regularized them, indicating what changes we have made. Price quite frequently phrases the winds differently from the strings, giving the winds a more legato line while the strings bow most notes individually. We have not tried to regularize phrasing between sections of the orchestra. Nor have we changed phrasing so that all the appearances of the same material will be phrased similarly; Price often phrases two appearances of the same material differently.

SOLO VERSUS À2

Price often does not indicate whether a woodwind line is to be performed by a single instrument or by both instruments together. Conventional wisdom here is that a solo instrument is more effective than two in unison; however, when Price does indicate her choice she seems to take the opposite view. The editors therefore tend to prefer unison doubling where there is no major benefit from assigning a line to a solo instrument. Price's own dispositions, which are often clear, have been respected throughout.

PRICE AND THE STRINGS

Price's scoring is, in general, straightforward, but she does have an idiosyncratic approach to string writing. Instead of viewing the strings as a five-part body (Violin 1, Violin 2, Viola, Cello, Bass) she views them basically as a body of four parts (Violins, Violas, Cellos, Basses), any of which may be employed either in unison or as two-part divisi. Thus, one of her favorite textures is unison violins accompanied by divisi violas and cellos (see Plate 2). This is a regular feature of all of Price's orchestral scores that we have been able to examine: both of the extant symphonies, the tone-poem *Mississippi River*, and the *Suite of Dances*. In sections of the first symphony scored for full orchestra, Price honors this form of scoring by writing Violas and Cellos on two staves throughout even when the part is in unison (and, since Price never uses the abbreviation "col primo," this makes for a great deal of work). The editors have opted to give Violas and Cellos a single line each in deference to the standard form of orchestral, score, indicating unison and divisi as needed. Quite often, she will write the violins on a single line.

The editors have assumed that this approach to string writing continues in the third symphony, where the strings are written out in their usual disposition. We have thus tended to assume that two-part viola or cello writing is divisi even when Price does not indicate such a division (which she seldom does) and when the part is technically playable as a set of double-stops. This decision is powerfully reinforced by the holograph Viola 2 part. It establishes all possible double-stops for the measures it contains as being in fact divisi. The very fact that Price prepared the Viola parts as Viola 1 and Viola 2 rather than writing out a general Viola part suggests the reliance she placed on divided violas. But this decision comes ultimately from experience with Price's string writing.

Accidentals

Price tends to let a single accidental serve for both voices when two parts are notated on a single staff. This is correct keyboard practice, but is dangerous for orchestral writing. This edition provides separate accidentals for each voice when two parts not in unison share a single staff, and accidentals added for this purpose are not noted in the Critical Commentary.

Dynamic markings

Price fairly regularly puts a dynamic marking between two lines of similar instruments (flutes, horns, violins, sometimes cello-and-bass), intending it to apply to both lines. This edition adds the missing dynamic markings, placing the added marking in square brackets.

Key signatures for the horns

Price follows the tradition that horn parts are written without key signature. In the opening measures of the first symphony, Price forgets that this practice will require her to add accidentals in the horn part for notes whose accidentals in other parts are covered by the key signature. By the horns' third entrance, in m. 37, she has begun to add the accidentals. Following modern practice, this edition adds key signatures to the horn parts.

Abbreviations

Price often uses the repeat-previous-measure sign; in this edition such measures have been written out in full. Price does not use abbreviations to indicate when one part is doubling another. When the parts have separate staves, she invariably writes out each part. In addition, she does not indicate that one set of measures is to be a literal repetition of earlier measures (in fact, she seldom repeats the scoring of a measure literally).

Percussion

Price's percussion notation is sometimes obscure. In particular, timpani and percussion often switch lines, sometimes in mid-measure. Furthermore, the key signature for the timpani part is inconsistent. She does not provide a key signature for the timpani in the first symphony, nor in the first two movements of the third symphony. However, from m. 6 of the third movement to the end of the third symphony, she provides a key signature. This edition provides a key signature throughout. When Price writes for a great deal of percussion, the individual instruments do not always hold to the same line; she seems to write for two sets of cymbals, one attached to the bass drum and a second set used for the occasional crash or plate roll.

Cathedral Chimes

The Symphony no. 1 in E Minor features a part for Cathedral Chimes (in the first movement, mm. 167–70; in the second movement II, mm. 215–47). The part for Cathedral Chimes was most likely written to make use of the Cathedral Chimes stop in the Echo division of the Roosevelt Organ in Chicago's Auditorium Theater, the location of the premiere performance. By 1932 percussion stops—especially chimes and celesta—were standard features of pipe organs; stops labeled "Harp" were also common, but they formed merely sub-octave extensions of the celesta. Price's training as an organist would have made her familiar with these resources. In this case, the chimes' primary advantage was their physical location in the Echo division in a chamber above the auditorium's ceiling. made the four ranks of pipes and the chimes sound "distant" from the rest of the instrument, and it allowed for spatial effects. We know that the entrance of the Cathedral Chimes was impressive in the first performance; when Price's friend Helen Armstrong Andrews wrote to her with congratulations on the first performance, her very first remark was "I was glad when the chimes were played."[2]

CRITICAL COMMENTARY

The commentaries for each work in this edition include the work's title, critical notes, and—where relevant—an explanation of editorial methods specific to the work at hand.

A series of successive pitches or note values are separated with an en-dash (–). Simultaneously sounding pitches are listed from bottom to top and separated by a plus sign (+). The Critical Notes use the following abbreviations: Bcl = bass clarinet; Bn 1, 2 = bassoon 1 or 2; BD = bass drum; Bns = bassoons; BTrb = bass trombone; Cb = contrabass; Cel = celeste; Cl 1, 2 = clarinet 1 or 2; Cls = clarinets; Crash Cym = crash cymbals; Cym = cymbal; Drs = drums; EHn = English horn; Hn 1, 2, 3, 4 = French horn 1, 2, 3, or 4; Hns = French horns; Hp = harp; Fl 1, 2 = flute 1 or 2; Fls = flutes; LH = left hand; Ob 1, 2 = oboe 1 or 2; Obs = oboes; Orch Bell = orchestral bells; PI = Piano I; PII = Piano II; Picc = piccolo; RH = right hand; SD = snare drum; Str = strings; Timp = timpani; Tpt 1, 2 = trumpet 1 or 2; Tpts = trumpets; Va = viola; Vc = violoncello; Vn 1, 2 = violins 1 or 2; Vns = violins 1 and 2. Pitches are indicated in the Critical Notes by the octave system CC–C–c–c'–c''–c''', in which c' represents middle C.

The Critical Notes describe the primary source at points at which editorial interventions have been made. The points of intervention are indicated for the most part by measure number(s) and the relevant voice or instrumental part. In some cases the critical note refers to a specific note within the cited measure; in cases where more specificity is required, the precise point of intervention is indicated not just by measure number but also by the number(s) of rhythmic notational element—counting only noteheads and rests, from left to right—within the measure. For example, the entry "74, Obs: . . ." would describe an intervention that involved the oboes, generally, in measure 74; the entry "95, Tpt 1: note 2, . . ." would describe an intervention that involved Trumpet 1 on the second note of the measure, and the entry "123.3–6, Vn 1: . . ." would describe an intervention that pertained specifically to the third through sixth rhythmic notational elements in measure 123 of the first violin part.

Symphony no. 1 in E Minor

The piano reduction that runs along parallel to the orchestral score is not complete, often skeletal, or not present at all. It has been carefully considered in preparing this edition, but it is not reproduced here. Variants between the piano reduction and the score are not documented unless they were deemed significant for the editing process.

Movement I

6, Bn: beats 3 and 4 are a quarter note followed by a quarter rest with fermata.

7, Hn 2: no sharp.

---

2. Helen A. Andrews to Florence B. Price, 19 June 1933. Florence B. Price Collection, University of Arkansas.

Wayne Shirley

7, Hn 4: note 3 has no sharp.

8, Hns 1, 3, and 4: beat 3 has no sharps.

9, Hn 3: note 1 has no sharp.

10, Hn 4: note 1 has no sharp.

10, Hn 3: note 2 has no sharp.

12, Va: F♯ (probably due to a momentary forgetting of the clef).

16–17, Vn 2: no tremolo.

18, Vn 1: no tremolo.

22–23, Hns: no indication that this is Hn 1 and 2 only.

22, Hn 2: note 2 has no sharp.

22, Vn. 1: no tremolo.

29–30: These two measures are a single measure in **1A**, with the notation at the top of the score "repeat this meas[ure] / accents 2ⁿᵈ time only." Price's numbering of measure from here on reflects that the repeated measures (m. 31 [end of page 5] and m. 32 [beginning of page 6]) have been renumbered from "30" and "31"; by m. 37 (end of page 6), however, the numberings reflecting the repeated measure are firmly in place.

31, Trb 3: note 3 is c.

32, BD: tacet.

39, Timp: *fff.*

40, Ob: note 2 is f♯′.

40, Hn. 3: note 3 has no sharp.

41, Hn 3: f♯′.

44, Vns, Va: note 7 has no natural sign.

48, Cl 2: note 2 is g♯′.

55, Vc: note 6 has both f♯ and a (slip corrected but not erased).

59, Cl: beats 2, 3, and 4 are blank (the repeat-previous-beat sign is understood).

60: Tempo marking is "A Tempo. Poco Meno Mosso." In **1A**, the horns hold over (until the downbeat) their notes from the previous two measures. In the photocopy that is the primary source of this edition, the string notes are corrected and indistinct. The winds clearly form a G major chord in second inversion; the piano reduction uses the indication "G I 6/4."

81–83, Cl: the notes are erased and crossed out.

88–89, Cb: the notes are crossed out.

91, Vn 1: note 3 is a quarter note, not a rest.

101: in the piano reduction, in PI, the g♯″ continues, and there is no sharp sign in m. 102.

105: in the piano reduction, the chord on the downbeat is B minor chord rather than E minor.

108–13: Fl, Ob, and Cl are on separate lines; m. 110 of the Fl line has the indication "Fl & Picc." In this edition, the Picc begins in m. 109, i.e., at the start of the phrase, rather than in m. 110 (with the entry of the brass).

108. Timp: note 6 is d.

109, Timp: A, dotted half note and quarter note.

111–12, Hn 1: a′, originally a♯′ in mm. 110–12, has been changed to b′ in m. 110 only, implying a change for the next two measures.

112, Trb 3: e.

113–14, Hn 3: no sharp.

114–17: source has a single line labeled "Fl./Pic./Ob." With "Pic" crossed out; there is no line for Cl. This edition continues Picc and Cl until m. 117.

116: The exposition does not lead back at all gracefully to the first measure of the piece. Since this repeat is unlikely to be taken by performers today, the editors chose not to construct a new version of the opening measure for the sake of the repeat.

117, Hn 3: no sharp.

117, Tpt, Trbs, Tb: *pp*.

127, Vn 1: ambiguous g′ or a′.

130, Bn: g (a in m. 131).

133, Vn 2: no sharp.

133, Cb: e (notated as F♯ in the piano reduction).

134, Trb 3: no note on downbeat; a whole note on e (for Trb 3 or Tb?) is erased.

135–36, Fl 1: erased, but not erased in m. 137.

136, Va: last note is a in the score but b in the piano reduction.

138–39, Bn 1: no flat.

145: in the piano reduction, in PII, the harmony is B♭7.

146, Cl 1: note 1 has no flat.

147, Cl 1: note 1 has no flat.

156, Vn 1: the dynamic marking *p* is erased.

171, Hn 1: note 3, no sharp.

171, Hn 2: no sharp.

171: piano reduction has b♭, but Vc has b.

172, Hn 2: g′.

179, Trbs and Tb: dynamic marking (probably either *mp* or *pp*) is illegible.

181, Hn 2: note 2 has no sharp.

182, Vn 2: primary source has no note in this measure.

186, Fl 2: beat 2 has three eighth notes without triplet bracket.

187, Vc: tutti.

187, Cb 1: measure is blank.

191, Cb 1: f.

193, Trb 3: no sharp.

193, Cb 1: no note.

198, Trb 3 and Tb: note 3 is a quarter note, not a rest.

201, Trb 1: note 1 is a quarter note.

210, Vns: note 5 is a quarter note.

212, Trb 1: no flat.

214, Cl 1: note 4 has no natural sign.

217, Bn: note 2 is f♯, written slightly high (crowded by the Cl part).

218, Bn: originally a dotted half note and quarter rest at the end of the measure, not erased.

220, Va: beats 3 and 4, alternating e′ and g′, are erased; nothing else is written in.

221, Trb 2: note 1 is g.

223–25, Ob 1: each falling semitone has a decrescendo.

Wayne Shirley

227, Ob: note 2 has no sharp.

227, Va: note 7 has no sharp.

229, Va: note 2 has no flat, and note 7 has no natural sign.

231, Vc 1: downbeat has no note.

233, Tpt: f′.

234, Cl: notes 4 and 5 are e″.

235–36: no part for Picc 2.

240, Tpt 1: beat 4 is ab′.

246: **1A** indicates "optional cut; bis" [i.e. play m. 246 twice] then 7 meas. out to 138 [= m. 254; Price starts numbering measures afresh at the beginning of the development]."

257–58, Trb 1: slur extends from m. 257, note 1, to m. 258, note 3.

260, Bn, Hns, Trbs, and Tb: half rest, quarter note with fermata, quarter rest; alignment suggests that these instruments play with Ob, Cl, and Tpt.

261, Timp: up-bow sign.

262, Timp: *fp*.

267, Cym: eighth note.

276, Cl 1: note 2 has no natural sign.

278–79: *dim.* erased in **1A**.

278, Cl 2: note 7 has no natural sign.

278–80, BD: there is no positive identification of this as BD.

280, Cl 2: note 1 has no natural sign.

284, Va: f♯′.

286–89: Picc alone retains "*cresc.*"; this is erased for rest of orchestra.

287, Va: no tremolo.

289, Va: no tremolo.

294–end, Hn 1 has no sharp.

297, Vn 2: half note (no rest).

297, Va: part includes e (in pencil m. 298, not present m. 299, ambiguous m. 300).

300, Trb 3 and Tb: *sf.* Erasures and revisions make this measure's complete history hard to decipher from the photocopy that is our source. The woodwinds and brass have a half note tied to an eighth note, while percussion and strings cut off on the downbeat. Above the score is an eighth note, staccato, with a tie reaching back to the previous measure; this seems to establish what Price finally wanted. It is possible that the fermata in the previous measure (notated only at the top and bottom of the score) also represents this later revision. Adding to the detail are sketched-in (pencil?) multiple stops for Vn 1 (g′+e″+b″) and an e for Va.

Movement II

6, Fl: no dot.

7, Fl and Cl: Originally these figures (and the figures in m. 14) ended with the third beat a quarter note followed by a quarter rest, similar to figures later in the movement (e.g., in mm. 69, 76, and 91). In mm. 7 and 14 Price erased the rest for Cl and changed the last note to a half note. Presumably she was following her occasional practice of changing the principal part and letting the copyist infer that the other parts were to be changed as well. In this edition,

Fls are extended to match the Cl in mm. 7 and 14; elsewhere, since conductors will probably want the note played as a *tenuto* quarter note, the figures is left as they appear in the manuscript.

11, Hn 4: note 2 has no sharp.

12, Hn 3: note 2 has no sharp.

12, Hn 4:, note 1 has no sharp.

13, Fl: no dot.

14, Fl and Cl: see comment for m. 7.

16, Hn 1 and 2: note 2 has no stems.

16, Hn 4: note 2 has no sharp.

18, Hn 2: dotted whole note d♯ (compare m. 80).

18, Hn 3: note 1 has no sharp.

18, Hn 4: note 2 has no sharp.

20, Trb 3 and Tb: no dot.

22, Hn 3 and 4: note 2 has no upstem.

28, Fl: no dot.

29, Fl: First note is a half note.

32, Tpt 2: note 5 is a quarter note.

36, Fl: a half rest occurs at the end of the measure.

51, Vn 1: no dot.

51–62, Vc: the editorial "*divisi*" extends until m. 58 (a new page), where Price marks "*div.*"

53, Va: no dot.

53–54, Cb: the measures are tied together (one measure off).

57, Bn: notes 1, 2, and 3 are quarter note, quarter note, and eighth note.

62, Vc 1: this measure has no notation; Vc 1 and 2 are on a single line until m. 104.

65, Hn 3 and 4: note 1 has no stem.

66, Trb 1: note 2 has no upstem.

67, Trb 2: First note is a dotted whole note.

71, Tpt 1: notes 4–5 are eighth notes (see also m. 240).

71, Trb 1: a line above staff may be a slur.

72, Hn 2: note 2 has no sharp.

72, Tpt 1: note 3 is a half note (there is no rest at the end of the measure).

73, Hn 1: note 2 has no upstem.

74, Hn 2: no dot.

76, Fls: notes are dotted whole notes.

77, Hn 3: note 1 has no sharp.

79, Hn 3: note 2 has no sharp.

79, Trb 1: notes 2–3 are eighth notes.

80, Hn 2: note 2 has no sharp.

83, Hn 1: note 4 has no sharp.

86, Hn 3 and 4: there is no indication that this measure is *a 2*.

93, Bn 2: note 3 has no natural sign.

94, Cl and Bn: notes 4–5 are eighth notes.

103–104, Hn 1 and 2, Trbs, and Tb: ties/slurs extend from m. 103 to m. 104 (new page); no ties/slurs back from m. 104 to m. 103.

110, Va 1 and 2: beat 3 has no natural sign.

112, Va 1: dotted whole note d'.

113–17, Va 1: an erasure in m. 112 has removed the alto clef from this passage.

117, Vc 1: no dot.

118–125, Bn: key signature has one sharp.

120, Trb 1 and 2: note 3 has no natural sign.

120, Trb 3: note 2 has no natural sign.

120, Vc 1: note 1 has no natural sign on f.

120, Vc 2 and Cb: no dot on whole note.

121, Cl 1 and 2, Bn: no dot.

123, Cl 1 and Va 2: no dot.

124, Hn 3 and 4: there is no indication in this measure that this is for Hn 3 only.

124, Trb 1 and 2, Vc 1 and 2: note 3 has no natural sign.

127, Fl 2 and Ob 2: no natural sign.

128–129, Cb: no natural sign.

129, Fl 2 and Cb: note 1 has no natural sign.

129, Hn 2: no dot.

129, Va 1: no dot on the a.

131, Fl 2: note 1 has no natural sign.

132, Ob 1 and Cl 1: no dot.

132, Bn and Trb 1: note 3 has no natural sign.

133, Bn: no dot.

137, Trb 1 and 2: note 1 is a half note.

139–55: On p. 49 of 1A, which contains mm. 133–40 of the second movement, the two oboe parts are written on two separate lines. Thus mm. 135–40, with each part written on its own line, are clearly for two oboes in unison rather than for a solo oboe. On p. 50 of 1A, which contains mm. 141–55, there is a single line for "Ob" and indication as to whether this is for one instrument or two. Since mm. 141–55 continue a major melodic statement that began in m. 139, there is a strong implication that this line should continue the scoring of mm. 139–40 and be for two oboes in unison. Nevertheless, the passage seems to be a classic oboe solo over light string accompaniment. While this edition accepts mm. 141–55 as being for Ob 1 and 2 *a 2*, the editors encourage conductors to consider the part from m. 139 as being a solo for Ob 1.

140, Ob: notes 4–5 are eighth notes.

145, Vc 1 and 2: no natural sign.

149, Va 1: no natural sign.

150, Ob: notes 1–3 are quarter note, quarter note, eighth note.

152, Ob: First rest is a quarter rest, followed by neither a dot nor an eighth rest.

155, Ob: beat 3 is a whole rest.

160, Cl: this measure contains both the designation *a 2* and a whole rest for Cl 1.

163, Bn: dotted whole plus half rest.

165, Bn: notes 1–3 are quarter note, eighth note, eighth note. This edition follows the piano reduction.

166, Cl: notes 1–3 are quarter note, eighth note, eighth note. This edition follows the piano reduction.

166, Va 2: no natural sign.

169, Vn 1 and 2: note 4 has no natural sign.

169, Va 2: note 1 has no natural sign.

169, Va 1 and 2: note 2 has no natural sign.

170, Ob: *pp*.

170, Cl: no dot.

174, Ob: no dot on the quarter rest.

174, Cl 2: no flat.

176, Ob: beat 1 has quarter rest, eighth note, eighth note. This edition follows the piano reduction.

178, Trb 2: G♮ (the natural sign is on the space for F; m. 179, has F (presumably F♮).

183, Hn 1: no sharp.

183, Trb 2: no rest at end of measure.

192, Timp: eighth note.

199–200: Vn 1 and 2 are notated on a single line in mm. 189–200; in mm. 189–198 they are obviously in unison; m. 200 has a separate part for Vn 2; m. 199 does not have rests for Vn 2.

204, Vn 1: notes 10–12 have no beam.

205, Ob: *tacet* until m. 206; the half note b′, following the piano reduction, seems logical by analogy with Fl in m. 207.

205, Cb: quarter note rather than half note; the quarter rest on the second half of the beat has been erased.

208, Fl: no dot.

210–53: On pp. 54–58 of **1A**, which contains mm. 201–49 of the second movement, the clarinet part is written on a single line marked "Cl"; except for the two-note chord in m. 209, there is no indication as to whether this is for one instrument or two. M. 209 begins a long, flowing, and rapid clarinet part that would seem to be for a solo instrument. However, on p. 59 of **1A**, which contains the last four measures of the passage, and on p. 60, which contains the end of the movement and an echo of the passage in mm. 259–62, Price writes parts for two clarinets, in unison, on separate staves. This edition there accepts the entire passage as being *a 2*.

212, Tpt 2: there is no note on the downbeat.

215, Hn 1 and 2: no dot.

216, Cathedral Chimes: note 2 has no natural sign.

218, Cl: beat 2 has *mf*.

219, Hn 3: note 2 has no sharp.

220, Hn 4: beats 2–3 have no rests.

221, Tpt 1: notes 3–4 are eighth notes.

223, Cl: notes 16 and 18 have no natural signs.

225, Cl: note 14 has no natural sign.

227, Hn 1: b′ dotted whole note.

227, Hn 2: d♯′ dotted whole note.

230, Tb: no dot.

232, Hn 3 and 4: note 1 has no stem.

232, Tpt 1 and 2: note 2 has no upstem.

232, Trb 1: notes 2–3 have no stems.

233, Cl: note 17 is e″.

233, Tpt 1 and 2: beat 3 has no stems.

239, Hn 1: note 3 has no sharp.

239, Trb 1 and 2: no bass clef (1A has treble clef for mm. 236–238).

240, Hn 2: beat 3 has no sharp.

240, Tpt 1: notes 4–5 are eighth notes.

241, Tpt 2: note 2 is a quarter note (the piano reduction establishes that this is a half note).

243, Cl: notes 4–6 have no beam.

243, Hn 1 and 2: note 1 has no stems.

243, Trb 3 and Tb: note 1 has no downstem.

255, Cl 2: g′ dotted whole note.

255, Hn 2: note 1 has no stem.

255, Hn 2: note 3 has no sharp.

Movement III

Percussion: At the top of the first page of the third movement, **1A** indicates "Dr[um]s—snare & bass, or small & large African drums." In this edition African drums are used through the middle of m. 80, snare and bass drums from the middle of m. 80 through m. 96 (where, except in m. 80, percussion is ad lib.), African drums in mm. 96–166 (except for the snare drum drag on the downbeat of m. 156, specified by Price), and snare and bass drum from m. 178 until the end (where Price has specified a snare drum).

Articulation of the main theme: As originally written (and as still in the reduction), the articulation of mm. 1, 5, 9, and 13 was as that of mm. 3 and 11, i.e., legato, without rests. Price went back and changed these figures throughout the piece. Occasionally, as in the oboe parts in m. 118 and the trumpet parts in m. 128, she forgot to change one line or set of lines. This edition adjusts those parts to match the articulation of the rest of the orchestra.

Violins: The violin parts in **1A** are notated on a single line through m. 64; they are also notated on a single line in mm. 103–10. At the beginning of the movement they are labeled simply "Violin," with no particular indication that Vn 1 and Vn 2 are to be playing in unison. On the page that begins with m. 33 the line is labeled "I–II." There is no label at all in mm. 103–10. This edition interprets all these passages as being scored for Vn 1 and Vn 2 in unison.

Possible repeats: In mm. 16–64 Price inserts a mid-measure double bar at the end of each eight-bar period. The double bars in mm. 32 and 40 have dots to the right that signify the beginning of a repeat; there are no corresponding dots to the left in mm. 40 or 48. Since mm. 40–48 is already a re-orchestrated repeat of mm. 32–40, this edition ignores the indefinite repeat signs.

17–32: Lower line of Perc has two notes (BD & Cym if SD/BD option is taken).

24, Trbs, Tb, and Str: note 1 is a quarter note.

47, Bn: beat 1 is an eighth rest.

64–65, Tpt: there is no slur, after the page break in **1A**, back from m. 65 to m. 64.

70: In **1A**, the rhythm of the upper winds is definitely two quarter notes, and the positioning in the measure suggest that Price wanted a disparity between the upper winds and the upper strings. Fl 1 and Ob 2 have tentative dots on the first quarter note; otherwise, the manuscript contains no hints of revision.

80, Hn 3: note 1 is a sixteenth note; note 2 is both an eighth note g♯′ and an eighth rest.

81–96: **1A** contains a line labeled "drs," but nothing is written in. Price probably intended to write the percussion part in later but did not. The fact that the timpani are playing here makes it unlikely that Price wanted the percussion to be silent. This edition realizes the percussion part lightly and takes advantage of the thinned texture to switch briefly to snare and bass drums.

97, Hns: tacet.

111, Va 1 and Vc 1: fermata.

112, Trb 3 and Tb: no upstem.

112, Cb: both *pp* and *mf* markings appear on the downbeat.

113–17, Perc: M. 113 of **1A** has a very faint quarter rest plus two eighth rests; mm. 114–17 feature equally faint repeat-previous-measure signs. This edition opts for Perc tacet in these measures.

115, Trb 1 and 2: this line is assigned to Trb 3 and Tb in **1A**.

117, Va 1: beat 2 is both eighth rest and dot from quarter on beat 1.

118, Ob: see "Articulation of the Main Theme" in general comments above.

126–27, Bn: tie (over page break) goes back from m. 127 to m. 126 but not from m. 126 to m. 127.

127, Hn 3: slur between notes 1 and 2.

128, Tpt: see "Articulation of the Main Theme" in general comments above.

129, Drs: beat 2 has three notes; **1A** notes both Drum lines on a single 5-line staff.

141, Trb 3: note 2 has no natural sign.

142, Hn 3: Hns 3 and 4 are unison in **1A**, but m. 143 (on a new page) is marked III.

147, Trb 1 and 2: on note 1, the chord has 3 pitches: a–c′–f′.

148, Va 1: no change to alto clef.

150, Trb 3 and Tb: note 1 has accent rather than staccato mark.

150, Va 1 and 2: note 1 is g′.

150, Vc 2: note 1 is g.

152, Timp: a note says: "or a′"; mm. 153–55 have only a.

153–55, Vn 2: as Ob (and transposed Cl) in m. 152–154 (one measure off cycle).

158, Hns: note 2 has d′+g′+b′+d″.

159, Ob 2: note 2 is eighth rest.

159, Va 1 and 2: note 2 has g″ and b″.

161, Trb 3 and Tuba: no downstems.

162, Cl 2: c″ half note.

165, Tpt: d′.

166, Tpt: c′.

167, Timp: tacet.

171, Vc 2: note 1 is both quarter note and quarter rest.

178, Tpt: measure has whole rest as b♭′+b♭″ half notes.

178–85, Perc (lower part): Price assigns this to either bass drum or large African drum, although starting in m. 178 the top line (which duplicates the lower part) is specified as being for snare drum. The lower line, however, does not have the *tr* sign of the upper line. This edition assumes that Price does not want the lower percussion part to be rolled.

179, Timp: no *tr*.

185, Picc: dotted quarter note and eighth note.

185, Hn 1: note 2, eighth note.

185, Hn 2: on note 2, there is neither a clear note head nor a connection between the sixteenth-note flag and the e″ of Hn 1.

186, Timp: both e and c.

Movement IV

7, Cl 1: downbeat, no dot on rest.

7, Cb: beat 2, no dot on rest.

8, Vc 2 and Cb: beat 2, no dot on rest.

14, Bn: no upstems.

16a, Bn: no upstem.

16a, Vn 1 and 2: beat 2 has a quarter note followed by an eighth rest (this was originally in Fl and Ob as well; Fl and Ob were changed by Price).

16a, Vc 1: no dot.

16a, Cb: *mf* on downbeat.

16b, Bn: no upstem.

16b, Trb 1 and 2: tacet.

20, Vn 1: no dot.

28, Cl 1 and 2: note 2 is dotted quarter.

32, Ob 1, Vn 1 and 2: no dot.

36, Fl 1: note 2 is dotted quarter.

41, Bn: no dot.

43, Cl 1: no dot.

50, Hn 2: no sharp sign.

54, Hn 2: no dot.

54, Vn 2, Va 1 and 2, Vc 1 and 2, Cb: beat 2 has no dot on rest.

56b, Hn 1 and 2: note 1 is b′+d″.

57, Ob 2, Cl 2, Hn 3 and 4: beat 2 has no dot on rest.

57–58, Trb 3 and Tb: no tie from m. 57 to m. 58; there is a tie back from m. 58 (on the next page) to m. 57.

64, Vc 1: no dot.

65, Trb 1 and 2: no dot.

67, Trb 1 and 2: no dot.

67, Tb: beat 2 has no dot.

68, Trbs and Tb: written in margin in **1A**.

68, Trb 3: no eighth rest at end of measure.

72, Timp: beat 1 has no eighth rest at end of beat.

76, Vn 1: beat 2 is a dotted quarter.

79, Va 1: beat 2 has neither a dot nor an eighth rest at end of measure.

82, Va 1 and 2: no dot.

87, Vc 2: no dot.

91, Va 1 and 2: no dot.

98, Hn 1: note 3 has no sharp sign.

98, Hn 4, Trb 3 and Tb: no dot.

100, Trb 1: no dot.

101, Hn 3: note 2 is quarter note and eighth rest.

101, Trb 2: no dot.

102, Hn 1: note 3 has no sharp sign.

104, Vc 1: fermata.

104, Vc 2: no dot.

110, Cl 1 and 2: no dot.

112, Va 1: note 2 is g.

114, Cl 1 and 2: on note 3, the flat sign seems to be incomplete.

130, Vc 1: no dot.

143, Tpt: instrument label is "Trpts."

151, Fl 1 and 2, Vc 1, and Cb: no dot.

170, Ob 2: no dot.

174, Bn 1 and 2: a+A.

174, Tpt 1: no dot.

174, Tpt 2: b′–a′.

175, Ob 1 and 2: quarter notes with eighth rests.

175, Va 1: on note 1, the upper note is d′.

181, Tpt: illegible.

190, Va 1: lower note is g.

192, Cl 2: note 3 has no sharp sign.

192, Vc 2: no dot.

193, Bn: no bass clef.

197, Timp: beat 2 has no dot on rest.

199, Timp: beat 2 has no dot on rest.

201, Timp: beat 2 has no dot on rest.

212, Vn 2: note 6 has no sharp sign.

217, Trbs and Tb: no dot.

220, Hn 3: note 2 has no dot.

220, Vn 1: note 3 is g″.

225, Hn 3 and 4, Trb 3, Tb, and Cb: beat 2 has no dot on rest.

230, Trb 3 and Tb: no dot.

236, Ob 2: no dot.

237, Tb: beat 2 has no rests.

240, Timp: note 2 has no dot.

262, Timp: dotted half–quarter rest–eighth rest.

263, Va 1: no dot.

268–69, Vc 2: duplets notated in terms of eighth notes.

269, Cb: beat 2 has no dot on rest.

273, Cl 1: no dot.

274, Cl. 1 and 2: duplets notated in terms of eighth notes.

Wayne Shirley

283, Ob 2: no dot.

284, Timp: no dot.

285, Fl 1, Tpt 2, and Vn 1: no dot.

286, Hn 1, Tpt 1, and Vn 1: no dot.

287, Cl 1 and 2, and Vn 2: no dot.

289, Hn 1: no dot.

290, Picc, Fl 1, Hn 1, and Tpt 2: no dot.

293, Hn 3 and 4, and Tpt: no dot.

295: tempo marking was originally "*A Tempo.*"

298, Perc: no eighth rest at end of measure.

314–16, Timp: no dots.

316–17, Cl 1 and 2: note 2 of m. 316 through note 1 of m. 317 is an octave higher.

318, Tb: beat 1 has no rests.

320, Picc and Fl 2: beat 2 is an eighth rest.

320, Fl 1: beat 2 is a dotted eighth rest.

320, Bn, BD, and African Drum: beat 2 has no dot on rest.

321–end, Hn 1 and 4: The disposition of the horns in m. 320 was originally that of mm. 321–24; Price moved the chord in m. 320 down to a lower, less blaring range. Given her habit of making a change in a first appearance and then not following up in later appearances, conductors might consider giving the horns the notes they have in m. 320 in mm. 321–24 as well.

321: Dynamics were originally *fff*, not changed in Vn 1 and Va.

321, Hn 1 and 2, Timp, Cym, and Va 2 (upper note): no dot.

322, Fl 2, Bn 1, Trb 1 and 2, Timp, Cym, Vn 2 (upper 2 notes), Va 2, and Vc 2 (upper note): no dot.

323, Fl 1 and 2, Bn 1 and 2, Trbs, Timp, Cym, Vn 2, Va 2, and Vc 2 (upper note): no dot.

324, Vc 1: blank.

Symphony no. 3 in C Minor

Movement I

11, Tb: note 1 has no natural sign.

12–13, Bn 1: slur across both measures.

14, Ob 1: note 4 has no natural sign.

22, Cl 2: note 1 has no augmentation dot.

30, Vc: no upstems.

32, Fl 3: note 1 is e♮".

32, Hn 1 and 2: note 1 has no upstem.

35, Bn: half note plus half rest.

35, Timp: f+a♭.

36, Ob: no upstem.

35, Va: *mp*.

38, EHn: *a 2*; note 3 has no natural sign.

40, Ehn: note 3 has no natural sign.

41, Fl 3: d♭.

41, Bn 1: e♭.

41, Bn: beat 1 is eighth plus eighth rest.

42, Trb 2: no half rest.

43, Cl: note 2 has no upstem.

45–52, Vn 1: The part is marked "soli" in mm. 45, with whole rests under the part (except in m. 52). This edition interprets the marking to mean "solo violin." A bracket at the end of m. 52 seems to indicate the end of the solo.

47, Cl 1: note 1 is f♯.

53–59, Vc: The part is marked "soli" in the top line and "div" in the other two lines. This seems to indicate a solo Vc accompanied by the section divisi, the section falling silent in mm. 57–58 where a single set of whole rests represents the resting section. There is no indication in m. 59 that the Vc line again represents tutti Vc, divisi, without the solo Vc.

54, Vc: no indication of nature of the divisi.

58, Va 2: a♭+c′ (double stop).

58–59, Tpts, Trbs, and Tb: ties back from m. 59, but no ties forward from m. 58 (across the page break).

61, Vlas: Final eighth note is B♮.

64, Fl 1 and 2: note 2 has no upstem.

64, Cl: note 3 has no upstem.

65, Fl 1 and 2: notes 2–5 have no upstems.

65, Cl: note 2 has no natural sign.

65, Trb 1 and 2: notes 3–4 are f♭–e♭.

67, Tpt 3: note 1 is c♭.

67, Va: notes 3–5 are slurred.

68, Hp, LH: no change to treble clef.

69, Hp, RH: b♮′+a♭″ (chord not filled in).

70, EHn and Cl: note 1 is quarter note.

70, Hp, LH: top note.

72, Va: note 4 is c′.

73, Cl 1: note 3 has no flat sign.

80, 84–85, Hp: no arpeggio sign.

84–85, Orch Bell: neither key signature nor flat sign on b′ and e′.

91, Trb 1: notes 1–2 are e♭–d.

91–92, Hn1: Source 3B has "Poco Rit." rather than "Rit." The marking starts in m. 92.

103, Va: note 2 has no downstem.

106, Ob: full measure slur as well as slurs included in this edition.

106, EHn: full measure slur.

107, Cl and Bcl: full measure slurs.

107, Hn 4: no flat sign.

108, Hn 3: c♭′.

108, Hn 4: b.

111, Orch Bell: neither key signature nor flat sign on e″.

133, Va 2: note 2 has no natural sign.

134, Fl 1 and 2: note 1 has no natural sign.

Wayne Shirley

136, Cb: beats 3–4 have neither note nor rest.

140, Bn 2: note 2 has no natural sign and note 3 has no flat sign.

140–141, Bcl: 3A is written an octave lower.

141, Cl: note 1 has no flat sign.

141, Vc 1 and 2: note 1 is dotted halves.

142, Bn 2: notes 1 and 2 are B♭.

142, Hn 1 and 2, Tpt 1 and 2: note 3 has no downstem.

143, Picc and Fls: note 2 is f′.

148, Ob: notes 4–5 have no downstem.

149, Fl 1 and 2: note 2 has no natural sign; there is no indication that beat 3 is for Fl 1 only.

152, Va 1: note 3 has no natural sign.

153, Va: notes 2–4 have no downstems.

153, Vc: beat 3 has no flat sign.

154, Ob and Vn 1: notes 2–3 have no upstems.

154, SD: Flams on beats 2–4 are written as double-stemmed quarter notes.

155, Trb 1 and 2: beat 4 has no upstem.

156, Tpt 3: note 3 is c♯″.

160, Vc 1: beats 3–4 have neither notes nor rests.

171, Fl 2 and Ob 2: note 3 has no flat sign.

171, EHn: note 8 is f′.

181–85, Perc (except for Tambourine): written on Timp line.

182, EHn: slur over notes 1–2.

183, Cl: note 4 has no downstem.

184, Ob 2: note 4 has no natural sign.

184, Cl: note 1 has no downstem.

185, Va 2: note 5 has no natural sign.

187–89, Hn 1: source **3B** has no tempo marks.

189, Va 2: note 5 has no natural sign.

194–95, Fl 1: solo only established in m. 196 by "I" marking.

194–96, Va: in source **3B** the rewritten section probably runs through m. 200. The oddly positioned chord on the downbeat of m. 201 is probably from an earlier version.

194, Cb: measure is blank in **3A**.

204, Cl 2: whole rest rather than half rest.

208, Fl: slur is over entire measure; note 4 has no natural sign.

210, Picc: beats 1–2 have dotted quarter plus seven beamed sixteenths.

212, Hp: marked "*Ped*" (=*lasciar vibare?*).

213–14, Vn 2: notes 5–12 have no *8va* sign (an *8va* sign in a similar spot appears in mm. 215–16).

218, Fl 1 and 2: note 4 is f‴.

218, Vn 1 and 2: notes 6 and 8 have no flat signs.

219, Fl 3: note 1 has a horizontal stress mark.

220, Cl: note 1 no flat sign.

220, Hp, LH: in the first chord the lowest note is C.

221, Bn: note 2 is e♯′.

224, Tb: flat sign rather than natural sign (a natural sign appears in m. 225).

225, Va: note 7 has no natural sign.

228–33, Va: a new page has a treble clef, but the notes are written as though in alto clef.

233–34, Tpt 1 and 2: slur over both measures; an additional slur appears over notes 3–4 of m. 234.

234–39, Bn: a new page gives bass clef (the notes must be in tenor clef in order to fit the harmony).

239, Va: source **3A** gives both treble and alto clef (the new page must be read as alto clef).

236–37, Trb 1: flat sign rather than a natural sign.

240, Cl 2: no note on beat 4.

241, Cl: no downstem.

241, Timp: note 2 is e.

253: Timp is on Perc line and Perc on Timp line.

253, Va 2: c♭.

Movement II

9, Vc 2: source **3A** has no part.

16, Vc 1 and Vc 2: stemmed together.

17, Vn 2: note 3 has no downstem.

26, Fl and Ob: fermata on note and rest (beats 2–3 are half rest in **3A**).

26, Fl 3: no natural sign.

27, Va 1: note 2 has no natural sign.

37–38, Va 1 and 2 and Vc 1 and 2: stemmed together.

41, Vc 1: beat 3 in half rest rather than eighth rest.

45, Cl 2: notes 1–2 are f′–a′.

54, Tpt 2: note 1 has no dot.

56, Trb 1: b♭.

60, Hp: no natural sign on d′ or d″.

60, Vc 1 and 2: stemmed together.

66, Trbs: there are four Trb lines in this measure. Trb 1 has c′–b–b; Trb 2 has d–b–b; Trb 3 has f♯–g–f♯; Trb 4 has d–d–f♯.

68, Fl 3: note 1 is e″.

70, Va: the downbeat is a+c♯′ (an octave below Vn 2), with both notes and accidentals written slightly high on their lines. Since beat 2 apparently has the same set of pitches with a fresh set of identical accidental signs, this edition reads beat 1 as b+d♯′, starting a parallelism of whole-tone chords that continues to the downbeat of m. 71.

71, Vc: note 2 has no natural sign.

75, Vc: no upstem.

76, Cl: half rest and quarter rest.

78, Va: note 1 is f♭.

78, Vc: no upstem.

81, Picc and Fl: second slur goes over entire measure; note 5 has no natural sign.

81, Cel, LH: beat 2 is blank.

81, Vn 2: note 1 has no stem.

82, Tpt 1 and 2 and Va: no upstem.

83, Cl: no indication of *a 2* until m. 84.

85, Hn 1 and 2: beat 3 is b′ quarter note.

85, Hn 4: note 2 is g′.

85, Tpt 1 and 2: notes 2–4 have no upstem.

85, Cel: note 1 has no dot on b′.

86, Ob: no indication of *à2*.

86, Cel: beat 1 is c♮″; beat 2 is d″.

86, Va: c♮′–e♯.

92, Vn 1 and 2: note 9 has no natural sign.

93, Vn 1 and 2: note 9 has no natural sign.

100, Bn: no bass clef.

100–101, Timp: no accidentals on any note (Timp line in **3A** has no time signature).

106, Fl 3: note 2 is g′.

108, Vn 1: note 4 has no downstem.

109, Vn 1: note 1 has no downstem.

110, Vn 1: note 1 has no upstem.

111, Cl: part is written on Bcl line, including indication for "I." and whole rest for Cl 2.

117, Orch Bell: no flat sign.

121, Ob 1: beats 2–3 have a♮′–a♭′ quarter notes.

121, Va 1: note 1 has no natural sign.

122, Cl: no whole rest for Cl 2.

124, Vc 1: note 1 has no stem.

129, Vc: no upstem.

135–end: Price's ties for the final tonic chord are not consistent. She seems to want the various sections of the orchestra to re-attack at different times (perhaps just to keep up the *forte* volume level rather than as a special effect). This edition attempts to systematize these re-attacks. Added ties are indicated as they are throughout this edition, by dashed lines. The one tie omitted is that for Hn 2 between mm. 137 and 138.

135, Hn 3 and 4: no dots.

137–40, Cl: a♭″.

140, Orch Bell: no flat sign.

Movement III

0–5, Timp: no key signature.

1, Timp: no flat sign.

3, Tpt 1: e′.

3, Va: note 4 is b♭.

5, Trb 2: note 2 has no natural sign.

6, Tb: tacet.

12, Bn: notes 5–7 have a slur over 3 notes.

14, Fl 1 and 2: note 2 is an eighth note (no rest).

18, Orch Bell: no flat sign.

21, Tpt 2: note 4 has no natural sign.

22, Vn 1: note 1 has an accent mark rather than an upbow sign.

28: tempo marking is "poco accel." in **3B**.

30, Trb 3: note 3 is f.

32, Vc: note 2 has no upstem.

35, Tpt 1 and 2: beat 2 has no downstem.

38, EHn: note 3 is a'.

41, Fl 1 and 2: notes 4–5 have no upstem.

41, Trb 3: double-stemmed.

43, Va: note 7 is g.

44, Fl 1: beat 1 has an eighth plus six thirty-seconds (no triplet brackets).

44, Vn 1: *dim.* mark in **3B**.

45: Several instruments that might be expected to carry out the cadential formula begun in m. 44 fall silent rather than reach for the new tonic. This seems intentional, not a slip by someone beginning a new section of music. This edition does not add notes on the downbeat of m. 45.

45: **3B** has mark for start of repeat.

46, Va 2: no flat sign.

47, Va 2: no natural sign.

47, Vc:, note 1 has no downstem.

50, Tpt. 1 and 2: note 2 is g♯'.

51, Trb 3: note 1 has no flat sign.

54, Vn 2: in the lower half of *divisi*, note 1 has no sharp sign.

57, Va: notes 2–5 have no downstems.

61, EHn: labeled "I" in **3A** with whole rest as though for EHn 2.

62, Fl 1 and 2: notes 3–4 are eighth notes.

63–64: In **3B**, Vn 1 is on Vn 2 line (copying mistake).

63–64, Vc: note 1 has no downstem.

64, Cl 1 and 2: note 2 has no natural sign.

66, Bn 2: note 1 is A.

69–71, Perc: the line given to Wood Block in this edition is identified as "wire brush & wood block." Since wire brushes are not particularly effective on the wood block, it is possible that Price first identified this line as "wood block," then wanted it as wire-brush snare drum, with the wood block taking the snare drum line for these three measures.

70, Ob 1 and 2: notes 2–4 have no upstems.

70, Vn 2: in the lower half of *divisi*, note 1 has no sharp sign.

71, Cl 1 and 2: beat 1 is tied to beat 2.

72, Bcl: note 2 has no natural sign.

73, Tb: no natural sign.

74, BD and Cym: empty measures.

77, Tpt 3: note 1 is e'.

78, EHn: *f* ⸻ before note.

85, Bn 1 and 2: note 5 is g.

Wayne Shirley

88, Trb 1: note 4 has no natural sign.

89, Va 1 and 2: note 2 has flat sign on Va 1 f′ rather than Va 2 d′.

90, Vc: notes 1–2 are g–f.

92, Tpt 2: no rest.

96, Cb: diminuendo.

101, Trb 1 and 2: beats 3–4 have whole rest.

105, Cl 2: note 1 has no natural sign.

111, Str: *p*.

111, Vn 1 and 2: note 3 has no natural sign.

114, Cl 2: no natural sign.

115–23, Trb 1 and 2: no key signature.

118, Bcl: no natural sign.

119–20, Trb 3: g♯.

120, Cl: not double stemmed.

126, Trb 1 and 2: not clearly *a 2* (previous measure is double stemmed).

127, Va: notes 1–4 are not double stemmed.

128, Vc: no upstem.

131, Fl, Cl: on beat 2 the rhythm is eighth–sixteenth–sixteenth.

132, Picc: note 6 is a′; slur extends from note 5 to note 6.

132, Trb and Tb: half notes are tied back to m. 131 in 1st, tacet in 2nd version of m. 132. (Second version = "133" in next note.)

"133": mm. 131–46 are in essence a more heavily scored repeat of mm. 115–30. Other than scoring, they differ only in that what was a single measure, m. 116, becomes two near-identical measures, mm. 132 and 133, in the repeat. The 2/4 sections of this movement move entirely in four-measure units except for the intrusive five-bar unit of mm. 131–35. M. 133, which occurs at a page break, seems to be simply a measure mistakenly scored again. There are even ties in the horn parts back to a rest in the second half of m. 132. Price has made a slip in recopying measures elsewhere in **3A**, although catching herself and deleting the extra measure. This edition omits m. "133."

133–34, Bcl: no natural sign in either measure.

135, Vn 1 and 2: slur between notes 2 and 4.

136, Cl: no upstem.

138, Vc: no upstem.

140, Cl 1: beat 2 is blank beat 2; part is realized from m. 124.

140, Bcl: blank; part is realized from m. 124.

143, Va: notes 1–4 have no upstems.

144, Hn 3 and 4: no upstem.

146, Picc: beat 1 is a quarter note.

146, Vc 1 and 2: stemmed together.

151–65: the percussion instrument that has the major solo in mm. 151–64 is identified as "Xylophone" at its entry and as "Marimba" at the start of the movement. Either instrument is usable, but this edition opts for the identification nearest the solo. In this part, Price uses her standard notation for percussion tremolo, which is *tr*; it seems clear, however, that the standard xylophone/marimba tremolo on one note rather than a whole-tone or semitone trill is what Price wants. In m. 151 Price notes that the clarinet part "can be used as solo substitute for xylophone," but in m. 151–57 this must apply to flute rather than to clarinet.

164, Ob: note 8 is a♮".

164, Vc 1: no natural sign on d'.

165–68, Perc: the Slap Stick line was originally for SD, with a note "for Snare Drum substitute (or add) slap stick for 4 meas[ures]." This edition substitutes Slap Stick for SD.

165, Timp: note 1 has natural sign.

168, Cl: slur for notes 3–4.

171, Cl: note 3 is b'.

175, Fl 1: note 5 has no sharp sign.

175, Fl 2: note 1 has no sharp sign.

175, EHn: the flat sign is in parentheses.

180, Hn 2: f'.

185, Cl: notes 2–4 are slurred.

186, Vc: note 4 has no upstem.

187, Fl 2: notes 2 and 3 are on Fl 3 line.

187, Tpt 1 and 2: notes 1–3 have no upstems.

187, Vc: note 1 has no indication that parts cross.

188, Hn 2: note 4 has no natural sign.

188, Tpt 3: note 4 is b♭'.

189, Vc: glissando line for Vc 1, the word "glissando" for Vc 2.

191, Cl: separate slurs for each beat.

194, Trb 1: no natural sign.

195, Bcl: in parentheses.

195, Va: the new page has alto clef but the part remains in treble clef.

Movement IV

1, Tpt 1 and 2: no downstem.

4, Tpt 1 and 2: note 2 has no downstem.

9, Cl: additional slur over entire measure.

11, Va 1: note 1 has no dot.

12, Cl: beat 2 has no downstem.

12, Vc 2: note 3 has no dot.

13, Ob: notes 2–6 have no downstems.

14, Vc 1: note 1 is g+b♭.

15, Bn 1: note 5 is B♭.

15, Bn 2: note 4 is B♭.

17, Tpt: rhythm is double dotted quarter–sixteenth–double dotted quarter–sixteenth.

17, Trb and Tb: rhythm is dotted quarter tied to dotted quarter.

18, Cl 1: note 5 has no flat sign.

18, Cl 2: note 2 is g'.

18, Trb 1:, note 1 has no dot.

Wayne Shirley

19, Tpt: rhythm is double dotted quarter–sixteenth–double dotted quarter–sixteenth.

20–21, Vc 2: missing (m. 19 has Vc 2 with tie to m. 20, at the start of a new page).

25, Vc 1: note 1 has no dot.

26, Trb 3: slur.

29, Trb 1 and 2: note 1 is both dotted quarter and eighth rest.

36, Vc 1: note 2 is c′.

37, Crash Cym: beat 1 has no rests.

42, Va: natural sign on Va 2 note rather than on Va 1 note.

43, Vc: notes 2–4 have no upstems.

50, Va 2: no natural sign.

58, EHn: natural sign.

61, Tpt: note 1 is quarter note plus eighth rest.

63, Ob 2: beat 1 has no rest.

63, Cl 2: a♭′.

64, Bn 1: note 2 has no dot.

65, Cl 2: no rest.

66, Ob: no downstem.

67, Fl 1 and 2: notes 2 and 3 have no upstems.

68, Cl 2: blank.

69, EHn: e♭′.

69, Cl 1: slur over notes 1–3.

69, Cl 2: dotted quarter.

69, Vn 1: double stemmed.

72, Cl 2: note 4 has no flat sign.

73, Cl: notes 2–3 have no downstems.

73, Cl 1: note 5 ha no flat sign.

75, Fl 1 and 2: notes 1–3 have no upstems.

76, Ob: no downstem.

76, Vn 2: note 4 has no natural sign.

77, Ob: note 3 has no downstem.

77, Cl 1: notes 4–6 have no slur.

82, Horn 2: f′.

93–100, Perc: SD and Cym seem to reverse lines in these measures. It is possible that Price wanted Cym rolls rather than SD rolls here, although this is not part of her regular style. It is also possible that she was thinking of the BD line as being for BD and Cym. In mm. 98–100, this edition interprets the line with the trill as SD and the bottom line as both BD and Cym.

96, Ob: note 2 has no downstem.

96, Bn 1: A♭.

97, Fl 1: note 2 has no dot.

99, Picc: note 6 is both b♭″ and e♭‴.

101, Bn: note 2 has no downstem.

101, Hn 4: no rest.

101, Tpt: note 3 is dotted quarter (no rest).

101, Va: note 3 is an eighth note.

103, Ob: note 4 has no downstem.

103, Ob 2: note 5 has no flat sign.

104, Ob 2: note 4 has no downstem.

105, Bn 2: note 1 is A♭.

106, Cb: dotted quarter (no rest).

107, Vc 1: note 4 has no flat sign.

108, Vc 1: note 4 has no flat sign.

110, Vc 2: G.

114, Hn 3 and 4: no upstem.

119, Cl 1 and 2: slur is over notes 1–2 only.

122, Fl 3: note 4 has no dot.

124, Hns: note 3 has no flat sign.

128, Tpt: note 4 is dotted quarter (no rest).

139: in this measure, which starts a new page, the EHn is written on the Ob line, and the Cl is written on the EHn line. Ob 1 and 2 do not appear; they are assumed to continue doubling the Fls. When Ob and EHn re-enter in m. 144, they are on their proper lines.

140, Cb: *mf*.

156, Cl 2: note 1 has no flat sign.

156, Bn 2: note 4 is c.

157, Bn 2: note 3 is c.

162–65, Perc: presumably SD, Cym, and BD are on the Timp line; presumably the Cym roll, on another line in m. 161, continues to be a plate roll instead of a stick roll.

164, Hn 1 and 2: flat sign is on f″ rather than e″.

165, Tpt 1: no dot.

166, Trb 1 and 2: no change to bass clef; tenor clef appears again in m. 167.

167, Bn 2: d′.

167, Hn 2: f′.

167, Va: note 3 has flat sign rather than a sharp sign.

171, Trb 2: note 1 has no dot.

182, Va, 2: no natural sign on a′.

183, Fl 2 and 3: no dot.

183, Hn 4: c″.

183, Va: no upstem.

184, Ob 2: note 4 is a♭″.

184, Tb: note 4 is G.

184, Va: notes 5 and 6 have no upstems.

185, Trb 1 and 2: note 1 is g.

185, Vn 2 and Vc: note 1 is dotted quarter (no slash).

186, Ob: notes 2–3 have no upstems, and notes 4–6 have no downstem.

188, Cl 1 and 2: note 3 is e♭′.

188–90, Trb 1 and 2: there is no change to bass clef for these measures. The pitch G is possible in m. 188, but m. 190 must be in bass clef, and thus it is likely that m. 188 is in unison with Trb 3 and Vc.

189, Cl: note 6 has no upstem.

190, Cl: notes 1 and 2 have no upstems.

190, Cl 2: note 6 has no sharp sign.

192, SD: no dot.

193, Ob: note 3 has no natural sign.

193, Tb: flat sign rather than sharp sign.

212, Ob: beat 2 is dotted quarter (no rest).

212, Tpt 3: note 1 has flat sign rather than sharp sign.

213: in **3A** this is marked "Rit." There is no other tempo marking until "Rit" again in m. 236. Perhaps there should be an "A Tempo" marking in m. 215. This edition opts for a consistent tempo, with no Ritard at m. 213.

219–20, SD: written on Cym line.

223, Tpt 2: note 3 has no flat sign.

223, Va 1: beat 1 has no slash on stem.

224, Va 2 and Vc 2: beat 2 has no slash on stem.

224, Vc 1 and Cb: no slashes on stems.

225, Hn 1: no flat sign.

226, Va 1: f′+a♭′.

227, Timp: g.

227, Tb and Cb: G.

227, Cb: no dot.

231, Va 2: note 3 has flat sign rather than sharp sign.

232, Va 1: note 4 is f.

232, Vc: not double stemmed.

236, Vn 2: no dot.

237, Tpt 1 and 2: note 1 is not double stemmed.

237, Tpt 1 and 2: note 2 is unison e♭″, not double-stemmed.

237–41, Timp and Perc: the label "Plate roll" is next to the Timp line; nevertheless, this line remains Timp while the second line of Perc is for Cym.

238, Tpt 1 and 2: note 4 has no upstem.

LITERATURE CITED

Primary sources

"Brief History of the Woman's Symphony Orchestra of Chicago," in Women's Symphony Orchestra Programs, Chicago Public Library, 1936–1940 (Chicago: n.p., n.d.).

Dett, R. Nathaniel. "Introduction." *In the Bottoms: Characteristic Suite for the Piano.* Chicago: Clayton F. Summy [1915], 1973.

"Florence Beatrice Smith Price." University of Arkansas, Mullins Library Special Collections. Manuscript Collection 988. Includes correspondence, musical scores, programs, photographs, and other papers, 1906–75. Gift of Florence Price Robinson and collected by Mary Dengler Hudgins and Barbara Garvey Jackson. Includes the Mary Dengler Hudgins Research Files.

Gaines, D. B. *Racial Possibilities as Indicated by the Negroes of Arkansas.* Little Rock: Philander Smith College, 1898.

"Mob Lawlessness: That Lynch-Murder and Burning at The Stake in Arkansas, Last Week, Inexcusable in a Civilized Country—Fear." *Cleveland Gazette,* 14 May 1927: 1.

Price, Florence. Symphony no. 1, E Minor ("1931–1932"). Photocopy of unpublished manuscript. University of Arkansas. Mullins Library Special Collections, Florence Beatrice Smith Price Materials.

———. Symphony no. 3, C Minor (1940). Unpublished manuscript (presentation copy). Yale University. Beinecke Rare Book Library, James Weldon Johnson Collection of Negro Arts and Letters.

"Prominent Colored Citizens of Central Arkansas." In *Biographical and Historical Memoirs of Pulaski, Jefferson, Ionoke, Faulkner, Grant, Perry, Garland and Hot Springs County, Arkansas.* Chicago: Goodspeed Publishing, Co., 1889.

Walden, Goldie M. "Keep Ideals in Front of You: They Will Lead to Victory, Says Mrs. Florence B. Price." *Chicago Defender,* 11 July 1936: 7.

Secondary sources

Beckerman, Michael. *New Worlds of Dvořák.* New York: Norton, 2003.

Block, Adrienne Fried. "Dvořák, Beach, and American Music." In *A Celebration of American Music: Words and Music in Honor of H. Wiley Hitchcock."* Edited by Richard Crawford, R. Allen Lott, and Carol Oja. Ann Arbor: The University of Michigan Press, 1990, 256–80.

Bonds, Margaret. "A Reminiscence." In the *International Library of Negro Life and History: The Negro in Music and Art*. Compiled and edited by Lindsay Patterson under the auspices of the Association for the Study of Negro Life and History. New York: Publishers Co., 1967.

Bone, Robert. "Richard Wright and the Chicago Renaissance." *Callaloo* 9, no. 3 (Summer 1986): 446–68.

Brawley, James P. *Clark College Legacy: An Interpretive History of Relevant Education, 1869–1975*. Atlanta: Clark College, 1977.

Brown, Rae Linda. "Florence B. Price." In the *International Dictionary of Black Composers*. Edited by Samuel A. Floyd, Jr. Chicago and London: Fitzroy Dearborn, 1999.

———. "William Grant Still, Florence Price, and William Dawson: Echoes of the Harlem Renaissance." In *Black Music in the Harlem Renaissance: A Collection of Essays*. Edited by Samuel A. Floyd, Jr. Knoxville: University of Tennessee Press, 1993, 71–86.

———. "The Woman's Symphony Orchestra of Chicago and Florence B. Price's Piano Concerto in One Movement." *American Music* 11, no. 2 (Summer 1993): 185–205.

Bullock, Henry Allen. *A History of Negro Education in the South from 1916 to the Present*. Cambridge: Harvard University Press, 1967.

"Coleridge-Taylor, Samuel." In the *International Dictionary of Black Composers*. Edited by Samuel A. Floyd, Jr. Chicago: Fitzroy Dearborn Publishers, 1999.

Crawford, Richard. *America's Musical Life: A History*. New York: Norton, 2001. Reprint 2005.

Dempf, Linda. "The Woman's Symphony Orchestra of Chicago." *Notes* 62, no. 4 (June 2006): 857–903.

Dietrich, Fred Walter. *The History of Dentistry in Arkansas: A Story of Progress*. Camden, Ark.: Arkansas State Dental Association, 1957.

Dillard, Tom W. "Scipio A. Jones: Fought Mobs, Climbed Rungs of GOP Politics." *Arkansas Gazette*, 30 January 1979: 4B. First published in *The Messenger* 10, no. 1 (January 1928): 10.

Ellison, Ralph. *Going to the Territory*. New York: Random House, 1986.

Epstein, Dena. "Frederick Stock and American Music." *American Music* 10, no. 1 (Spring 1992): 20–52.

Faxio, Lorraine M. "The Music Program of the Works Progress Administration: A Documentation and Description of Its Activities with Special Reference to Afro-Americans." In *More Than Dancing: Essays on Afro-American Music and Musicians*. Edited by Irene V. Jackson. Prepared under the auspices of the Center for Ethnic Music, Howard University. Westport, Conn.: Greenwood Press, 1985.

Freer, Eleaner Everest. "Discrimination Against American Music." *Musical Leader* 66, no. 26 (13 October 1934): 22.

Gatewood, Willard B. *Aristocrats of Color: The Black Elite, 1880–1920*. Bloomington: Indiana University Press, 1990.

———. "The Formative Years of William Grant Still: Little Rock, Arkansas, 1895–1911." In *William Grant Still, A Study in Contradictions*. Edited by Catherine Parsons Smith. Berkeley: University of California Press, 2000, 21–38.

Gomery, Douglas. "Movie Palaces." In *The Electronic Encyclopedia of Chicago*, 2005. Chicago: Chicago Historical Society. Available at http://www.encyclopedia.chicagohistory.org/pages/850.html.

Graves, John William. "Negro Disfranchisement in Arkansas." *Arkansas Historical Quarterly* 26 (1967): 190–225.

———. *Town and Country: Race Relations in an Urban-Rural Context, Arkansas 1865–1905*. Little Rock: University of Arkansas Press, 1990.

Green, Mildred Denby. *Black Women Composers: A Genesis*. Boston: G. K. Hall/Twayne Publishers, 1983.

Holly, Ellistine Perkins. "Black Concert Music in Chicago, 1890 to the 1930s." *Black Music Research Newsletter* 9, no. 2 (Fall 1987): 6.

Horowitz, Joseph. *Classical Music in America: A History of Its Rise and Fall.* New York: Norton, 2004.

Hull, Gloria T. *Color, Sex, and Poetry: Three Women Writers of the Harlem Renaissance.* Bloomington: Indiana University Press, 1987.

Lamb, Earnest. "From Spiritual to Symphony: A Portrait of Florence Price." Radio broadcast transcript dated February 1993, in Price Materials, University of Arkansas.

Ledbetter, Steven, and Victor Fell Yellin. "George Whitefield Chadwick." In *The New Grove Dictionary of American Music.* Edited by H. Wiley Hitchcock and Stanley Sadie. London: Macmillan Publishers, 1986.

Locke, Alain. *The Negro and His Music.* New York: Arno Press and the *New York Times* [ca. 1936], 1969.

McSwain, Bernice Lamb. "Shorter College: Its Early History." *Pulaski County Historical Review* 30 (Winter 1982): 81–84.

Neuls-Bates, Carol. "Women's Orchestras in the United States, 1925–45." In *Women Making Music: The Western Art Tradition, 1150–1950.* Edited by Jane Bowers and Judith Tick. Urbana: University of Illinois Press, 1987, 349–69.

Northup, Solomon. "Twelve Years a Slave," 1853. In Eileen Southern, *Readings in Black American Music*, 2nd ed. New York: Norton, 1971, 93–102.

Paine, Lewis. "Six Years in a Georgia Prison," 1851. In Eileen Southern, *Readings in Black American Music*, 2nd ed. New York: Norton, 1971, 88–92.

Pettis, Ashley. "The WPA and the American Composer." *Musical Quarterly* 26, no. 1 (January 1940): 101–12.

Smith, Dr. James H. *Maudelle: A Novel Founded on Facts Gathered from Living Witnesses.* Boston: Mayhew Publishing Co., 1906.

Southern, Eileen. *The Music of Black Americans: A History*, 3rd ed. New York: Norton, 1997. Referenced in text, 2nd ed., New York: Norton, 1983.

———, ed. *Readings in Black American Music*, 2nd ed. New York: Norton, 1983.

Spivey, Donald. *Union and the Black Musician: The Narrative of William Everett Samuels and Chicago Local 208.* Lanham, Md: University Press of America, 1984.

Still, William Grant, as told to Verney Arvey. "My Arkansas Boyhood." *Arkansas Historical Quarterly* 26, no. 3 (1967): 285–92.

Terry, Adolphine Fletcher. *Charlotte Stephens: Little Rock's First Black Teacher.* Little Rock: Academic Press of Arkansas, 1973.

Tick, Judith. "Passed Away is the Piano Girl: Changes in American Musical Life, 1870–1900." In *Women Making Music: The Western Art Tradition, 1150–1950.* Edited by Jane Bowers and Judith Tick. Urbana: University of Illinois Press, 1987, 325–48.

"Whispers of Love: A History of the R. Nathaniel Dett Club of Music and Allied Arts, 1922–1987." Unpublished typescript.

White, Shane. "The Stroll." In *The Electronic Encyclopedia of Chicago, 2005.* Chicago: Chicago Historical Society. Available at http://www.encylopedia.chicagohistory.org/pages/121.html.

Wilson, Olly. "Black Music as an Art Form." *Black Music Research Journal* 3 (1983): 1–22.

———. "Composition from the Perspective of the African-American Tradition." *Black Music Research Journal* 16, no. 1 (Spring 1996): 43–51.

———. "The Significance of the Relationship Between Afro-American and West African Music." *The Black Perspective in Music* 2, no. 1 (Spring 1974): 3–22.

Yenser, Thomas, ed. *Who's Who in Colored America*, 4th ed. (1933–37), 5th ed. (1938–40), 6th ed. (1941–44). Yonkers-on-Hudson, N.Y.: C. E. Burckel.

Young, Percy M. "Samuel Coleridge-Taylor, 1875–1912." *The Musical Times* 116, no. 1590 (August 1975): 703–705.